DIAGNOSING THE SYSTEM

for organizations

The Managerial Cybernetics of Organization

'We are aware that the many techniques of cybernetics, by transforming the control function and the manipulation of information, will transform our whole society.

With this knowledge, we are wide awake, alert, capable of action; no longer are we blind, inert powers of fate.'

Pierre Trudeau
Harrison Liberal Conference
21st November 1969

The Managerial Cybernetics
of Organization

DIAGNOSING THE SYSTEM
for organizations

Stafford Beer

Companion volume to

BRAIN OF THE FIRM
and
THE HEART OF ENTERPRISE

JOHN WILEY & SONS
Chichester · New York · Brisbane · Toronto · Singapore

Reprinted August 1988
Reprinted June 1990
Reprinted April 1991

Library of Congress Cataloging in Publication Data:

Beer, Stafford.
    Diagnosing the system for organizations.
    Includes index.
    1. Organizational effectiveness.   2. Communications in
organizations.   I. Title.
    HD58.9.B44   1985   658.4′02   84–25795

    ISBN 0 471 90675 1

British Library Cataloguing in Publication Data:

Beer, Stafford
    Diagnosing the system: for organizations
    1. Organization
    I. Title
    302.3′5   HM131

ISBN 0 471 90675 1

Printed and bound in Great Britain by
Biddles Ltd, Guildford and King's Lynn

DEDICATED TO

Ron Anderson
Mary Lee Brassard
Martine Chomienne
Lyle Emmott
Susan Francis
Andrew McAusland
Bob McNutt
Wamuyu Ngechu
Laura Winer

'Why, a four-year-old child could understand
this . . .

Run out and find me a four-year-old child.'

Marx

CONTENTS

WHAT THIS BOOK IS

This book presents a new way of looking at ORGANIZATIONAL STRUCTURE — whether you are interested in a firm, an international conglomerate, a social service, a consortium of like-minded people, a government department, or a national economy . . .

Hitherto, the approach to organizational structure has had only one tool: the 'family tree' organization chart. Typically, this chart has been frozen out of history: it is geological genealogy! Things have got like this because events (inventions, markets, opportunities, entrepreneurs, capitalists, workers, economic environments, glory and misery, all intervening) led to this, and not to something else. The organizational structure has been rationalized — *after* the event. And there it sits, offering the manager its own explanation of how things actually work.

But — as the manager well knows — this arbitrary organization chart has little to offer him beyond a procedural method for **blaming somebody** for whatever has gone wrong. It is not enough. To apply simple rules to the chart, such as the one that says only seven people should report to one person, may help to reduce the chaos. And of course there is a vast management literature that bears on the problems that the whole business generates.

The fact is, however, that there is a whole science having to do with the manager's own prerogative: TO ORGANIZE EFFECTIVELY. It is called cybernetics, and a note about that will be found a few pages further on.

The point about this book is that it should *guide* any manager through the questions that affect his own organizational structure, in the light of cybernetic science, without requiring of him or her any prior knowledge at all of this difficult interdisciplinary subject.

i

As you thumb through the book you will realize that it looks like nothing that you have wrestled with before. There is no need to be discouraged by that: and at the least it means that something new is happening.

The same is true of the Handbook that goes with the simplest domestic appliance, the audio-system, the video-recorder, the personal computer, these days. The Handbook reduces the electronics to diagrams. This book reduces cybernetics to diagrams.

Your hi-tech Handbook will also have to introduce a few technical terms. It points to switches, and names them. It will tell you about special facilities that you may or may not have encountered before. This book does the same — and it gets by with *less than twenty* technical terms, most of which you will more-or-less know already.

There is a big difference, however, between this guide and the hi-tech home Handbook. No-one expects that the Handbook will show you HOW TO DESIGN the system that it describes. This book *will* tell you how to design an organizational structure — *and* HOW TO DIAGNOSE a faulty one.

Now that is a large claim. So please do not expect this brief manual also to reflect on matters of psychology, of social anthropology, of industrial relations, and so on. It is not that they are excluded, not that I disregard them. A lot is implicit in this book that derives from these fields; and even I have written about them in detail elsewhere. But we cannot tackle everything at once.

This also goes for the problems of *measurement* and *filtration* that are dealt with in the last two books mentioned opposite. The aim here is to consider ORGANIZATIONAL STRUCTURE itself, in the shortest posisble compass consistent with the range of input available from cybernetic science and the manager's own grasp of novel ideas.

The books that have been published before this one all have some relevance to the approach encapsulated here. The first five are:

Cybernetics and Management, English Universities Press, London, 1959 (ten languages)
Decision and Control, Lanchester Prizewinner, John Wiley, Chichester, 1966 (also in Spanish)
Management Science, Aldus Books, London, 1967 (several languages)
Platform for Change, John Wiley, Chichester, 1975
Designing Freedom, The Massey Lectures, John Wiley, Chichester, 1976 (also in Spanish and Japanese)

But the companion volumes issued, as is this, under the general heading of *The Managerial Cybernetics of Organization*, are:

Brain of the Firm (first published by Allen Lane in 1972, and available in several languages) in its *Second Edition*, much extended, John Wiley, Chichester, 1981
The Heart of Enterprise, John Wiley, Chichester, 1979.

It is to these last, in particular, that the reader is referred for more elaborate explanation, and above all for the **justification** of statements that are made here without proof (although such statements, once made, tend to be intuitively obvious — like other truths). No other references are given in this book, because the last two, *Brain and Heart*, are the sole sources of the model developed in this one. Sources that lie behind the model are of course listed in the other books.

All this is said for the sake of good order . . .

This book is meant to stand on its own, and to be fully accessible to the manager who will spare the time to work through it. There is, however, no reason why he should not lighten the task by taking a staff aide into his confidence, as he might do in making any other study.

S.B.

INTRODUCTION

In Montreal there is a University called Concordia — a remarkable place in many ways. Professor David Mitchell, one of the pioneers of cybernetics in Canada, headed the Graduate Programme in Educational Technology. In June and July 1982 he assembled a group of mature post-graduate students of diverse backgrounds to study the cybernetics of organization with me.

The Minister of Education in Quebec has decreed that a credit system should be used, each representing 45 hours of study. Our activity was to count as three credits — 135 hours in all, of which 24 hours was officially accorded to teaching. As things turned out, 35 hours was spent in class, and there were individual tutorials as well. With the necessary private study, the assignments, and the written work, most of the participants must have put in far more time than that allocated. Judging by the results, some must have put in double.

The first of the attractions to me in accepting this professorial residency was to find out how a formal system like this would work. I have taught this material for years in both Britain and the United States. There have been many individual post-graduate students who have specialized in managerial cybernetics, and there have been many managers in many countries who have worked zealously on their own projects. But not before this Concordia experiment (nor since) has the viable system model been taught *for examination*, still less for *explicit credit* to a higher degree. In Manchester University, for example, where I have taught at my home base (the Business School) since 1969, such an arrangement as was implemented at Concordia is unthinkable. It would disturb the status quo in the faculty — where novel ideas are enthusiastically encouraged and promoted — to alter the balance of the examinations. It has to be admitted that there are no more than a hundred percentage prints in a whole square hat, although I am sure that the faculty would add a few more if they could for cybernetics.

The second attraction to me in undertaking this mission was to find out — within this rigorous format — what difficulties people have in understanding this material. Obviously, there has been plenty of advice of the kind that is hurled from the touchline. Disgraceful, said one reviewer of *Heart*, that it contains no references. But it does. This sort of help doesn't help, in short. The fact remained that all sorts of people who were not merely showing off in reviews were saying nervously: 'yes, but how exactly do we proceed?' It seemed obvious to me — but it could not have been obvious: there was an articulate need for this very guide. Since I did not know how to write it — just what it was with which folk had difficulties — I asked the Concordia students to tell me.

This they did. After all, many were teachers themselves — back to chew things over, and to obtain their higher degrees. But they were *also* people who had already experienced the role and responsibility of management, in diverse enterprises. I asked them not to pull any punches — and they did not. So we almost failed to get started at all. Later, the honesty brought us all close to desperation several times. Did it help, or not, that every classroom session was video-recorded? 'Heisenberg Rules — perhaps.'

Along with the nine registered students, various others were involved. David Mitchell, naturally, was the central pivot. Observers from the university were also involved, including to varying degrees a number of the faculty. One of these in particular, Richard Schmid, worked so hard and with such synergistic effect, that I wish that he had made his doctorate out of it — but he had the thing already.

Teams were formed, on the understanding that a team could consist of one up to nine people. They were due to discuss, *severally and generally*, a range of explicit viable systems.

In the event, and with David and Richard participating, seven such systems were chosen by the group. The University itself, and a manufacturing industry, were obvious starters. The Health Service of Quebec Province not surprisingly came next. The choices of a third world Broadcasting Corporation and an international organization for planetary protection were not so predictable. *The Family* should not have been, but was, quite a surprise. Finally, the recursive embodiments of **language** as a viable system took us from philosophy through linguistics to anthropology and back again.

The range of these examples was deliberately large, as was the sharing of results. So I am not associating people with their own primary projects. The students gave me permission to quote their work — but I do so only implicitly. Readers of this book will find themselves invited to 'take a large sheet of paper'. Some of the records from Concordia are two metres high. As it is, the material is unpublishable — though any one of the seven case studies would make a good book.

This book is the result of *my* learning; but please do not blame the Concordia folk if I have got it wrong. I told them that if it ever got written, it would be dedicated to them. It has taken a long time, because I spent an intervening year in Mexico trying to apply these ideas, as I had done a dozen years earlier in Allende's Chile. But democracy in Mexico is not about casting votes, but counting them . . . So: here we finally are. The dedication has been written, for the nine people who actually earned their grades — coupled with the names, as toastmasters say, of David Mitchell and Richard Schmid — with a little quotation that I hope will remind them of the tussle.

My own recollections will remain fresh, because of the loving friendship of these people. A certain professor from New Brunswick, none other than Bob McNutt, wrote in his last paper for me:

> 'There are more things in your philosophy, Horatio, than we have time to consider right now.'

Beautiful.

FOREWORD

CYBERNETICS
AND MANAGEMENT

'Science has sought the ultimate source of energy in the physics of the sun itself . . . the hydrogen-helium fusion. Science now seeks the ultimate source of control, in the cybernetics of natural processes ` . . . the brain itself.'

from *Cybernetics and Management*, Beer, 1959

Cybernetics is the science of effective organization.

The eminent mathematician Norbert Wiener wrote the first book on the subject in 1948, and gave the classic definition (though he did not object to my later one). It was:

the science of communication and control in the animal and the machine.

First def.

The first line of this definition indicated the primacy of the role played by **information** in regulatory systems: in fact, it was later mathematically proved that such a system must necessarily contain a representation (or model) of whatever is being regulated. But this was by no means obvious forty years ago; and the realization by the founders of cybernetics that the *feedback* of information is ubiquitous in regulation for every sort of system was a major scientific discovery.

It leads us to the second line of the definition, which points to the existence of laws or principles of control that apply to all kinds of complex systems, whether animate or inanimate, technical or societary. This is a major allegation in the ears of most people. We were brought up to focus on the *differences* between men and machines, between individuals and groups. There are whole branches of science that thrive on these differences, and do not want to know about the similarities — still less about the underlying *identities*.

ix

Worse than that: the distinctions that were drawn between these various kinds of system, for reasons not specially connected with regulation, carried with them strongly emotive — even ideological — connotations. The result is that people hold all sorts of beliefs about such potent issues as freewill and determinism, freedom and oppression, economic good and social justice, that are buttressed by scientific distinctions that are out of date. Many of them, indeed, in the light of contemporary cybernetics, enshrine erroneous conclusions, which is worse than being merely unhelpful.

Well, management is — if you will — the *profession* of regulation, and therefore of effective organization, of which this cybernetics is the science. So obviously the findings of the science should be made fully accessible to managers. This does not in the least deny that other sciences have relevance to management: of course they do. From economics to psychology, from anthropology to mathematical statistics, every science has an 'applied' side that bears on the management process.

In this book, you are invited to apply the findings of cybernetic science solely to the question of **organizational structure**. Yes, I know that there are many other aspects to management: I was a manager myself for about twenty-five years. However, if the structure is dysfunctional, then no amount of financial wizardry, of insightful man–management, of business technique, will save the day. Increasingly, it seems to me, the organizational structures we inherited **do not work**. We shall see why.

THE VIABLE SYSTEM

'The laws of viability lie at the heart of any enterprise. So too do human beings.'

from *The Heart of Enterprise*, Beer, 1979.

When people refer to the firm, or any other institution, as 'viable', they are often referring to economic viability. From this preoccupation with the economic dimension stems the assumption that most of our problems are economic too.

Solvency, it is true, is a prerequisite of business activity — to trade while insolvent is illegal. Profitability, too, is a prerequisite — lack of business confidence is not illegal, but it is lethal. So these affairs are of primary concern. But they do not (as many suppose) constitute the *goals* of the enterprise. Rather are they the *constraints* under which it operates. So of course the regulation of cash-flow (for example) is an important managerial concern. And of course profit-consciousness in the private sector, or the consciousness of social benefit in the public sector, has to apply to expenditure; and proper returns on capital are required.

However: the tendency in 'the city', and among financial journalists, to treat all this as the essence of viability, is to mistake the epiphenomena of the system — the appearances and flurries of activity that prove it is actually there — for the system itself. Which of the firm's workers, or even middle-managers, could recognize the old place by its indices of ROI, P/E ratios, and the rest? These things are *abstractions*, and very useful ones too, if we want to manipulate successfully our economic constraints.

My point is not that abstractions are unrealities, but that there is more than one set of them. This book offers a different set of abstractions as a working tool.

The laws of viability in complex organisms are not merely, or even primarily, concerned with the energy (like the metabolism of money) that propels them, but with the dynamic structure that determines the **adaptive connectivity** of their parts. Can the organization actually survive — *assuming* that the financial constraints are met?

As to managerial problems: these are no respectors of financial boundaries, nor of the territorial preserves of any other professional function or geographic domain.

They grow like cancers; and 'secondaries' may appear anywhere. The organization as a viable system has to become immune to infection, adaptive to environmental change, and — somehow — to extirpate its cancers.

THE DIAGNOSTIC ENQUIRY

> 'People are happy to add to the pharmacopoeia; they forget to swallow the medicine.'

from the *Lindsey Sutcliffe Memorial Lecture*, Beer, 1982

So the book is going to develop, with your intimate collaboration, a Model of the Viable System — the one that concerns you in particular. Since the very word 'viability' has a basically biological significance, there need be no inhibition about viewing this as a *diagnostic* enquiry.

As we put together the anatomy of the viable system, then — be ready for it — we shall be able to notice that bits of it may be missing. As we discuss the physiology of the viable system, also, we shall be able to recognize those functions that are not operating effectively.

- Some subsystems do not work too well.
- Some inter-connexions are too formal or too informal.
- Some communication channels cannot carry their due informational loads.
- And so on —
  IN PARTICULAR:
  the balance of central direction and local autonomy may be 'trying to disobey' the cybernetic 'Law of Cohesiveness', thereby inducing stress.

Do not these diagnostic indications make sense already? The 'in particular' surely represents a syndrome wholly recognizable by any manager — or, for that matter, any citizen . . .

Then please think positively about the discoveries you will make, and make the diagnosis FOR ACTION as you go along. People really do make a practice (see the Sutcliffe quotation above) of **recording remedies** in their files. The thing to do, when you have recognized the remedy required, is to hold your nose, open your mouth, and **swallow**!

CONCERNING RESULTS

> 'Rather than to solve problems it is clever to dissolve them.'
>
> from *Decision and Control*, Beer, 1966

One of the main reasons why so many problems are intractable, is that they are formulated in such a way as to defeat any solution.

We go on trying the solutions that have always failed to work in the past, instead of attempting to pose the problems in a different and solvable way.

> Example? — they are all around us. Here's one.
> Everyone knows that the penological system does not work, produces socially disastrous consequences, and is quite absurdly expensive. It is a system for educating criminals in crime, at a cost greater than we spend on educating our own children.

Well then: you must not expect the Walls of Jericho to fall down just because you blew the trumpets.

The way you are likely to get results out of this book — and they are sitting there for the taking — is to arrange the organizational structure differently, and to put its procedures in cybernetic order (that does not mean revising the paper work).

The problems that were worrying people will then be not so much solved as dissolved.

This means that you will not get any credit.

This FOREWORD is over — so:

FORWARD ...

THE
VIABLE
SYSTEM

§ ONE

VIABLE:

able to maintain a separate existence

— *The Oxford English Dictionary.*

An organization is viable if it can survive in a particular sort of environment. For although its existence is *separate*, so that it enjoys some kind of autonomy, it cannot survive in a vacuum.

The foetus is called viable at the moment when it is *able* to 'maintain a separate existence', which is long before it is actually born. And afterwards, the individual maintains ties with mother and family, with a locality, with a culture . . . existence is never independent of other existences, even though the individual has a separate **identity**.

In the same way, other sorts of organization have identity, and are capable of independent existence, even though they can survive only within a supportive environment. A village is a recognizable and viable organization, with its church and its school, its butcher's and its baker's: but it is embedded in a rural society that nourishes it, and in a larger social system beyond that which underwrites its cultural identity.

Similarly, a firm may be the subsidiary of a larger corporation: it is a viable entity in itself, but in a specially defined way it 'belongs' to (what is often called) the 'parent' company. Its wealth-generating profit centres likewise 'belong' to it — although they *could* be hived-off, and sometimes are.

In using this Viable System Model, or VSM, it is therefore important first of all to determine precisely what is the organization to be modelled, and to specify its boundaries — although these may well change as the organization adapts.

Next, you will need to specify its viable parts, and the larger viable system of which it is itself a viable part. This takes some disentangling, and time and thought should be devoted to the task.

The big problem is this:

> you are not determining absolute facts:
> you are establishing a set of conventions.

So remember:

> a model is neither true nor false:
> it is more or less useful.

Then will any sort of description of the organization suffice? No indeed. In particular, the standard 'family tree' is quite unhelpful — except to establish who is ultimately to blame if things go wrong! This is because the organization chart makes no attempt to model VIABILITY.

THIS SKETCH
depicts a viable system in rough outline.

But take a close look at it. The total system contains two systems which are identical with it. Like the foetus mentioned earlier, these two embedded systems are themselves viable systems.

They are RECURSIONS OF THE VIABLE SYSTEM. We shall make use of this mathematical term because, while its meaning in context is evident, it reminds us that we are not talking loosely about **any** kind of system contained inside another — but about an absolutely precise definition of viability.

Please look moreover at the large dotted square, and note that its content is identical with the red structure in the two lower recursions. This is because the dotted square is a basic component of the **next higher** viable system.

2

A ROUGH SKETCH
OF THE MODEL
OF ANY VIABLE
SYSTEM

Rough it may be —
but do notice
that it is
mathematically
exact ...

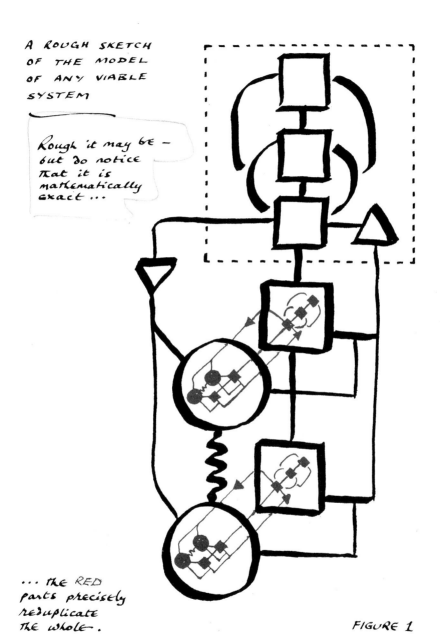

... the RED
parts precisely
reduplicate
the whole.

FIGURE 1

3

Maybe your study of this initial sketch provoked the thought that this version has no connexion with the outside world. Correct: we shall turn to this omission repeatedly. Meanwhile, however, the diagram highlights a most important feature of viable systems: they are **self-referential**. Their logic closes-in on itself. In this characteristic lies the explanation for

- the maintenance of identity
- the facility of self-repair
- self-awareness
- recursivity itself.

It is worth reflecting on the potency of this arrangement, and on the fact that recursions of the viable system can be extended upward to the terrestrial globe (within the Universe) and downward to the cell (containing molecules, containing . . .). In practice, the best plan is to consider a trio of viable systems at any one time: the organization we wish to study, that within which it is contained, and the set of organizations contained by it — **one level of recursion down**.

Look again at the diagram on the last page to take this point fully:
the sets of viable systems shown in red themselves contain viable systems, and so on down. But we shall concern ourselves with the red ones ALONE.

Hence, if the viable systems contained within the red organizations call for explicit discussion, the methodology proposes that we shift the whole trio of recursions to which we are attending one recursion down.

Then the organization that we originally decided to study becomes 'the next higher recursion', the contained red organizations are now of primary concern, and the blobs-and-boxes lost within the red organizations now emerge as 'the next lower recursion'.

Think this through in detail with the help of the facing diagram — there are four triple-recursion projects shown, each one focussing in RED on an organization one recursion removed from its neighbour.

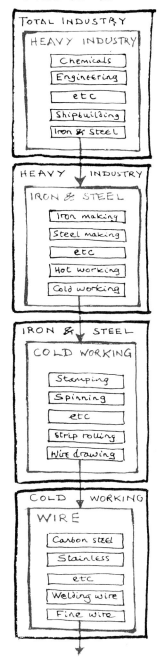

FIGURE 2

POINTS TO NOTE

- Each of these four squares ought to be envisaged in terms of the VSM sketch already studied.
- How we specify the whole series and its elements is a matter of choice, of utility to our purpose.
- There is no hierarchic significance in the vertical listing of elements. These may be strongly or weakly connected.
- ◄— In this case, the strong connexion is actually sequential.
- Let us re-affirm: any one organizational study will focus on the RED SQUARE. It will take into account this system's embedment in the higher recursion of the big (black) box, and the content of the five (arbitrarily five) small boxes embedded in it. The connectivity between levels of recursion is a major topic of our study . . .
- . . . for the moment it is surely exciting to note that (just as the VSM is always the same) the connectivity between **any** pair of recursions is the same.
- The saving in time in analysis, diagnosis, computerization — induced by this invariance — is enormous.
- ANY ORGANIZATION, although quite properly depicted as belonging to 'THIS' set of recursions, belongs to an arbitrarily large number of other sets of recursions too. For example, Iron and Steel also breaks up geographically, or by Companies.

5

NOW DO THIS:

You are a viable system. In which viable system are you
embedded? How many recursive systems can you list
before you reach some kind of 'totality'?

> This is to cast your own self in the role of 'fine wire'
> in the comparable tabulation of industry we just
> examined — and to work upwards.

Please make some kind of diagram, so that these ideas
become familiar and a record of your investigations is
begun.

Experience suggests that you may well have found it difficult to
decide which chain of systems you wanted to model. You belong
to a family, which belongs to a village, and so on (that chain was
mentioned earlier). But you also have a job — which embeds you
in a firm or a service or whatever. The chain of systems is now a
different one. You belong perhaps to a church, to a sports club, to
an 'old school' — and so forth. Each of these chains of systems,
which embed each other and ultimately you, we can call a
recursive dimension.

Whatever viable system we wish to model exists in a variety of
recursive dimensions. 'What business are we in?' is the classic
question for a board of directors to consider — and there may be
several answers. So the SYSTEM-IN-FOCUS may have more than
one next higher and next lower recursion. It can be thought of as a
viable system that is central to a whole sphere of existence: the
sphere is marked out by a collection of recursive dimensions
running through the system-in-focus at the centre (as the rim of a
wheel is marked out by its spokes).

Had you forgotten the admonition at the foot of the previous page
in doing this exercise?

Although it is important to develop an easy familiarity with recursive dimensions, and with the shifting of the system-in-focus to another recursive level, there will be no need to make all the possible mappings implied by the whole 'sphere of existence'. To the contrary: the whole point is that one should correctly choose the triple embedment on which to work. Usually it is obvious enough that certain named entities constitute the system-in-focus, and the next higher and next lower recursions. It is only a proper appreciation of dimensionality (as just defined) that permits a most-useful determination of systemic **boundaries**.

- In the experiment just undertaken, how did the dimensions of your own existence affect the boundaries of the systems of higher recursion that you were able to specify with exactitude?

   (That is, did you get your legal self mixed up with your vocational self, your religious self, your aesthetic self, and so forth?

   Since the integral you is the system-in-focus, a perfect identity of all these selves is ideal — at the centre of the sphere.

   But in terms of **management**, the way in which a life is conducted, dimensionality becomes important: many psychiatric problems are rooted in inter-dimensional conflict that is not understood because boundaries have not been recognized.

   The same goes for your firm.)

- Secondly, in the completed experiment, when you reconsider all the organizations nominated, are you certain that each one is actually a viable system as defined?

7

Let's remember that a viable system is capable of independent existence . . .
　　. . . within a specified environment.

Human beings are perfect examples of viable systems — BUT suck all the air out of the room, and then see how viable they are.

On the other hand, the viable system is necessarily a **producer** of the organization, and not just an adjunct to it, however important. An invoicing department has no meaning unless the product is there to be invoiced; and it would surely be perverse to contend that it is a viable system whose environment is the whole corporation.

NOW DO THIS:

Think of a manufacturing company known to you as the System-in-focus.

List the organizations of the next lower recursion — that is, the embedded subsidiaries or departments that between them PRODUCE THE COMPANY.

These are all to be viable systems in themselves. They are essentially profit centres. They can in principle be 'hived off' — sold as going concerns (and replaced by bought-in products or services).

Next make a list of company systems or departments that are NOT embedded viable systems.

It is important to spend time on this exercise. Most of the incorrect inferences (and therefore the inopportune diagnoses and recommendations) made in applying the VSM derive from nominating activities that are not in themselves viable systems as if they were.

Look back to Figure 1 and observe that many structures are shown that are NOT red embedments — viable systems in themselves. This exercise begins the process of discovering what they might be.

Please do some writing or diagram sketching before turning the facing page. The notes on self-reference may however aid the thinking process.

About Self-Reference

Mention was made earlier of the self-referential nature of viable systems: Their logic closes in on itself, we said.

This is not to say that a viable system is a closed system: we shall soon be studying its ecology — environmental interaction with an 'outside'.

For the moment however, all the emphasis is on what the biologist calls the **internal environment**.

All of the systems that are not next level recursions are dedicated to STABILIZING this internal environment. The biological name for this stability is HOMEOSTASIS.

> For example, in the body:
>
> While the heart, lungs, liver, kidneys and so on are all engaged in *producing* the organism, other supportive systems are dedicated to the homeostatic functions of keeping the temperature stable, maintaining the blood sugar level, managing water levels, balancing hormones . . .
>
> Similarly, in the firm:
>
> While the profit centres produce the company, cost control, quality control, management inventory, stock control — all these are obvious examples of homeostatic regulation, and financial accounting generates the *balance* sheet after all.

But as you do the exercise on the facing page, some activities ought to give you pause. What about the Board, the sales division, the engineers, the computer department, for instance?

This notion is likely to be wholly unfamiliar: try to understand it. Self-Reproduction is usually thought of as the outstanding characteristic of viable systems. But it is continuous and regenerative self-production that underwrites IDENTITY.

How did the exercise go?

One thing that may well have become obvious is that classical organizational formulae, such as 'production, sales, finance' cannot be of much help in thinking through the structure of a viable system. It is wholly unsafe simply to list major departments (however essential, however powerful) as constituting the next lower level of recursion.

Here are some comments on typical problem areas, as mentioned on the preceding page:

The Engineers

Assuming that this is not an engineering *company* (making turbines or switchgear or boilers), 'the engineers' are probably engaged in maintenance and in designing and making special purpose bits and pieces of machinery.

The Company could not operate without them, yet they are not a viable system. Their job is to facilitate operations — not *any* operations, but *these* operations.

Now here comes a vital distinction. The engineers could form themselves into a guild of jobbing engineers, resign as a body, and set themselves up as a contract maintenance outfit. This little company would be a viable system. The distinction is this: the men and their joint engineering expertise can be 'hived off' in this fashion — but they do not take their function, the works' orders and the plant modus operandi with them. They take their knowledge of such things, but not what they actually **do** in the firm.

This example makes a gentle start, because these folk do not often think of themselves as 'separate existences'. This is not usually true of the next group of people.

The Sales Division

In fact exactly the same considerations apply to sales as to the engineers — assuming that the company is not a selling concern entire. There certainly are companies that buy in goods, and then sell them, and do nothing else. In that case, to sell is to produce the company.

In a manufacturing concern, however, the sales function **facilitates** the passage of goods from the viable units that make them to the consumer. Obviously, this activity is focussed on the market-place; and the whole operation takes place altogether **outside** the domain of Figure 1 (although it is necessarily anchored within it).

Certainly the sales function is vital — so is the body's endocrine system — but it is not normally a next recursion viable system.

> NOTE: So the Sales people were absolutely in order when (relatively recently) they began to say that they discharged a MARKETING FUNCTION.
>
> No doubt it sounds better to be a Marketing Director than a Sales Manager: this time the instinct has survival value.

The Computer Department

After entertaining these two considerations, the case of the computer (which often causes great dissention) will surely fall easily into place.

Once more we have a **facilitator**: it is a unit intended to make things happen more smoothly and more quickly. And once again we observe that the computer group may leave as a group, and set up shop as a viable system — as a bureau or as a consultancy. But they cannot take the stuff of their computing with them. To take the data relating to company management would be absurd as well as illegal; to take the software would be far from absurd and is usually done, but it remains theft. However, distinguishing between software created for the employer's ownership and the programmer's files of personal knowledge is beyond the competence of the legal system (which has not begun to address such matters non-trivially so far).

Next: if the firm is bold enough to have a computer unit that is concerned not merely to facilitate more smoothly and quickly, then its activities will necessarily be concerned with innovation instead. This innovation will either be directed to managerial ends (for example, in simulating alternative policies) or it will

11

spawn a computer-based activity that might become a subsidiary company — and therefore a viable system itself. In either case, the computer department is not a viable system in its own right.

Finally comes the special case, which does occur. Just as there are companies for which engineering or selling *are* (atypically) activities that produce the company, so are computer bureaux viable systems. Now it may happen that a firm constitutes its own facility as a bureau — which sells its output. If this product, or part of it, goes to an outside customer, then — if it is significant — it may best be regarded as an embedded viable system. If the product is 'sold' only internally, under transfer pricing, then this is merely conventional. In such a case, as in the internally-used component of the general bureau case, the unit is not a viable system — especially insofar as it has no exposure to market forces. Transfer price systems simply do not work when there is external (and probably cut-throat) competition.

The Board

> The Board cannot possibly be a viable system . . .
> The Board is a subsystem serving internal and external homeostasis.

Not all Boards know this.

The outstanding problem in considering the role of the Board is tied up with the self-reference characteristics of the viable system. Whose power does the Board embody? The law says that of the shareholders. But the Board also embodies the power of its workforce and its managers, of its customers, and of the society that sustains it. The Board metabolizes the power of all such participants in the enterprise in order to survive. If it fails in this, the participants will use their power against the so-called viable system out of selfish interest: to keep wages up, to keep prices down, to preserve the ecology — depending on their roles. It is a fascinating feature of contemporary society that the participants (all those mentioned) seem willing to pursue selfish interest to the point where the viable system in which they have a profound stake, as employees, as needy consumers, as regional inhabitants, is actually rendered viable no longer.

If neither the participants have understood the viable system, nor the Board has recognized systemic self-reference, then the identity — the survival — of the enterprise is under threat. It always was; but people used to behave in ways that were consistent with viability most of the time. That they do so no longer results from the increased social awareness of the underprivileged, at home and throughout the world, the archaism and disuetude of the civil and moral law, and the general incomprehension of technological advance.

The **redesign** of institutions, from firms to governments, from educational establishments to social services, is the end to which survival-minded people must address themselves. If the process does not start with properly constituted Boards, it will start (as we observe) with 'alternatives' — many of which (as we also observe) involve violence.

It may be that your interest is to model an organization quite different from a manufacturing company. Unfortunately, it is not feasible to run through all the kinds of organization that there are. But if the organization is a viable system at all, it will contain lower-recursion viable systems that **produce** it. Identify them; and do not be bullied by current practice or power politics into including subsidiaries or units as viable systems when their roles are supportive rather than productive of the System-in-focus.

In particular, the argument that this treatment 'does not apply to us' is always spurious, because the approach concerns only those factors that are **invariant** in all viable systems. The biggest red herring of all among these false contentions is the one that claims 'we do not make a profit'. That makes no difference to the structure of viability at all. True, it poses problems of measurement, and the fixing of criteria of success: these will be discussed later. But a hospital or a school or a government department has to produce itself, continuously and regeneratively, to maintain the identity that it has — just like any other viable system.

13

Choices about embedments will still have to be made, and they will be based on insight into the viable system and the judgment of utility in the emergent model. For instance, what **produces** a university is its acitvity in teaching and research (and not its elaborate hierarchy of a court, a senate and a hundred committees, its famous library, its accommodation and catering facilities). But whether the teaching and research are embodied in viable systems called faculties, with embedded departments, or in courses, with embedded options, depends on the model maker. S/he might ask the question: which account is more conducive to the need for adaptation? It is often worthwhile to develop more than one model, and to learn from its elaboration.

Elaboration there certainly will be. On the facing page you will recognize the model of total industry, and of its one embedded viable system heavy industry, that we used before. Last time we picked out iron and steel — and analysed that industry through a couple more recursions. In doing so, obviously, we discarded the remaining elements of each level of recursion, because they did not belong to the System-in-focus. The new diagram stops at the second level of recursion, and graphically illustrates how the viable systems proliferate in the horizontal plane. The picture is presented to help you 'get the feel' of modelling in this mode . . .

. . . and please do not blame the theory of viable systems for making life so elaborate, because life *is* that way — but especially because this approach is in fact a **simplifier** of elaboration. The point was made before about the vertical recursion: all the embedded systems, and all their embedments, and so on, all have the SAME structure. Now even the horizontal spread of replications, at every level of recursion, is seen as having that same structure too.

It is beyond argument that 'total industry' is very large and very elaborate. No amount of ingenuity can make it less so. What science CAN do, however, by finding the invariances that underly viability, is to make all of it susceptible to a uniform description. Contemplate this, then, through the eyes of Figure 1:

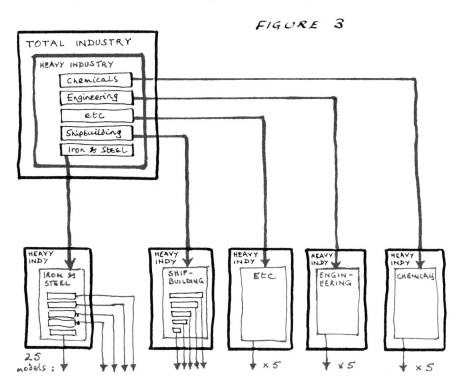

FIGURE 3

Very large viable systems indeed, such as the marine and fisheries administration of Canada, such as the whole social economy of Chile (in Allende's time), were modelled in this way — in less than two years. It is all due to the **parsimony of natural invariance**.

Probably you will not need to take advantage of the widespread (that is, vertical and horizontal) invariance of viability structures by mapping everything in sight — even within your own organization.

Even so, it is an excellent plan to envisage the whole organizational terrain in these terms before narrowing down to the specifics of the model that you intend to construct. This will give you a comfortable sensation of knowing where you are in relation to major features of the territory, and some confidence that you are using a useful descriptive language of general application in this zone. (It is all too easy to talk in the esoteric terms of an inherited nomenclature that beg the vital questions.)

NOW DO THIS:

Choose and clearly define the System-in-focus that you intend to model.

Survey the sets of recursions of viable systems that constitute its organizational 'ecology', both vertically and horizontally.

Give the System-in-focus a well-chosen name.
(This is not altogether easy. It is vital to distinguish THIS system from all its embedments, and from its organizational 'cousins' in the horizontal plane.)

Exactly specify, with a name, the viable system in which your system is embedded.
(If there is more than one of interest, do the job twice — and distinguish between names.)

Exactly specify, with names, the viable systems that your System-in-focus embeds.

You know, after this, precisely what you are doing in terms of a triple recursion: the System-in-focus is in the centre of a higher level of recursion, in which it is embedded, and it contains a set of viable systems which exist at the next lower level of recursion.

SPECIAL TERMS OF § ONE

VIABLE   *able to maintain a separate existence.*

RECURSION   *a next level that contains all the levels below it.*

SELF-REFERENCE   *property of a system whose logic closes in on itself: each part makes sense precisely in terms of the other parts: the whole defines itself.*

HOMEOSTASIS   *stability of a system's internal environment, despite the system's having to cope with an unpredictable external environment.*

INVARIANT   *a factor in a complicated situation that is unaffected by all the changes surrounding it (such as the speed of light or the value of π).*

§ TWO

The best place to start work is the embedded viable system of the System-in-focus. Let us pick it out of Figure 1, like this:

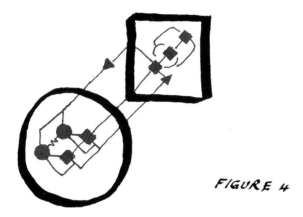

FIGURE 4

The red diagram is the sign of the viable system, and the black components belong to the System-in-focus. We shall start here because it is this part of the viable system that **produces** it. Of course, your list of embedments will contain more than one subsidiary (Figure 1 contained two of them, and you might have up to seven or eight: not many more, I hope, or else you may be missing a whole level of recursion).

The **set** of these embedments will be known as SYSTEM ONE of the System-in-focus. Each component, such as the one above, will receive the same treatment as the others.

19

To come to methodological grips with the problem of analysis, the first of our actions is to **cut out** the red part of the picture. Get rid of it. This leaves for consideration simply a black square and a black circle. Leaving aside the fact that this does not leave much for us to work with (but there is!), please pause here long enough to answer this question — which has a precise and important answer:

PLEASE REPLY TO YOURSELF

Why is the red portion of Figure 4 to be eliminated from consideration?

The answer is that *this* is not the System-in-focus. The red infrastructure exists at a lower level of recursion than you decided to consider.

> If this was not your own clear-cut answer to the above red question, then the meaning of systemic recursivity is eluding you — it would be advisable to return to the previous section.

CONVENTIONS:

For ease of reference to other writings about the viable system, we shall keep to the diagrammatic conventions that have been in use for twenty years.

The square encloses all the managerial activity needed to 'run' (whatever that may mean)

the circle, which encloses the relevant operations that *produce* the (total) viable System-in-focus.

The amoeboid shape represents the environment of all this, which — until now — has been kept in the background.

The red arrows refer to the necessary interactions between the three basic entities: each stands for a multiplicity of channels whereby the entities affect each other.

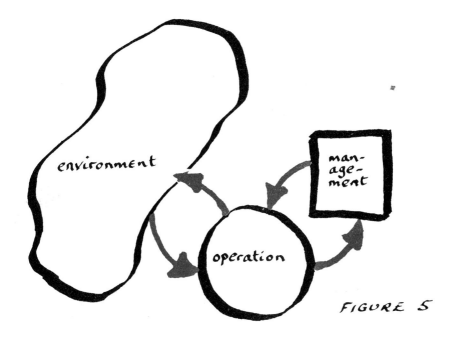

FIGURE 5

What can possibly be done with the picture at Figure 5, given that it is inadmissable to consider the infrastructure discarded from Figure 4? It comes down to asking what is really going on in the dynamics of any enterprise.

Perhaps what is going on is the manipulation of men, materials, machinery and money: the four M's. Yet there is a more fundamental manipulation that occurs: it applies to the biological cell as a viable system, as well as to a giant corporation, or to a government.

What is going on is the MANAGEMENT OF COMPLEXITY.

In order to discuss this, a special term is enrolled. It offers a *measure* of the complexity with which management has to deal.

The term is **VARIETY**.

Variety is a measure of complexity, because it counts the number of possible states of a system.

21

You may well say that the number of possible states in a complicated entrepreneurial system is not precisely countable. That is surely correct. However, it is countable in principle: it is therefore amenable to the making of *comparative* statements (this has *more* variety than that), and to the arithmetic of *ordinal* numbers (this product is the *fifth* most profitable).

Adopting this extremely practicable usage straight away, we can state that the square management box has lower variety than the circle that contains the operations. This is evident insofar as no management can possibly know **everything** that happens. For example, this morning Bill (who was operating the third machine on the left as you go in the third bay after No. 7 Gate) had a row with his wife, and fumbled about in getting the work started — a four-minute set-up time took six minutes. It is a 'possible state of the system'; but you did not know that it happened, and it is not even listed as a possibility.

We can safely go on to assert that the (circular) operational system has lower variety than the environment. For example, we manufacture our kitchen equipment in eleven different colours (there you are, then: you *can* sometimes measure variety exactly); but this morning a lady asked for heliotrope with yellow spots. You did not know this — and now you do know you will not do anything about it: uneconomical, you say.

So the basic axiom will assuredly hold, that the variety of the environment greatly exceeds that of the operation that serves or exploits it, which will in turn greatly exceed the variety of the management that regulates or controls it.

Then what anyone would expect to happen does happen. The clues to this are visible in the two examples just recounted.

HIGH VARIETY is necessarily cut down, or attenuated, to the number of possible states that the receiving entity can actually handle.

On a diagram, it is useful to mark the high-variety input with the (electrician's) symbol for an

attenuator

to show that variety is being balanced (remember *homeostasis*) to the variety that the receiver can accommodate.

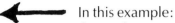 In this example:
the works' manager is not going to bother about these small matters that make for high variety in the lives of those working on the shop floor. They are **filtered out**.

NOTE: Computers are able to capture, store, **and deliver** more data than will go into your head.

> BUT ANSWER THIS:
> Is designing an attentuator of variety the same thing as jettisoning data?

In this example:
the marketing manager knows that he cannot expect his retailers to stock more than a small range of colours. They are artificially reduced in number.

NOTE: In spectroscopic terms, the chemist is able to generate more distinguishable colours than the human being can distinguish!

> BUT ANSWER THIS:
> How do you design the attenuator of variety — by telling the chemist to be quiet?

These examples of variety attenuation belong in our diagram like this:

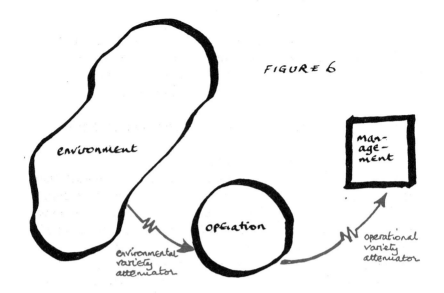

FIGURE 6

ANSWERS:

As to operational variety attenuation, it is a big mistake — easily made — to confuse data with variety (closely related as they are). Data are certainly distinguishing possible states of the system, but they are generated by/through classifications, categories, definitions . . . **These** determine variety, and **these** are within our power to design. If we do not design them, a common fault — especially given computers — attenuation JUST HAPPENS. The brain and the managerial culture between them will filter-out what variety is left-in beyond the capacity to assimilate.

Typical example —

a machine-shop has three bays, containing 22, 47 and 31 machines. Allowing for all possible variations of width, thickness, quality and so forth, there are 40,000 possible products. The work-study people have been at this, to handle pay-and-productivity. The cost accountants, too, calculating standard costs, computing variances. It is all in the computer.

Managers often allow themselves to be inundated with this lot, but they undertake variety

24

attenuation surreptitiously, peeking at totals and budgets. Or they may boldly ask only for moving averages on each of the three bays. Then they suddenly discover the relevance of quality . . . or something else.

As to the example from environmental attenuation, the answer to the question is:

by *market research*.

Many people suppose (without much thought) that because market research 'finds things out' it must be an *amplifier* of *managerial* variety. Maybe this sometimes happens: information about new technology, for example, may increase the number of managerial options. But in the case quoted, the idea is to reduce the impractical and uneconomic expression of demand to a range (variety = eleven in this case) that the works can handle.

REMEMBER :
The *lethal* variety
attenuator is
SHEER
IGNORANCE
!

SUPPOSE, however, that market research repeatedly advises that the market is looking for *fourteen* colours . . .

SUPPOSE, however, that labour negotiations keep stumbling over something that is *not* in the computer: a general dislike of some particular combination of production orders, for example . . .

25

Now two problems have been generated, one by each of our completely different examples. But in terms of **variety engineering** (as the manipulation of varieties by design may be called) they are identical. An *invariant* has emerged.

NOW ANSWER THIS:

What would you first of all try to do in each situation?

What is the INVARIANT FACT that links the two examples, and is represented by the *single* question mark completing the previous page?

ANSWER:

The invariant is the fact that each attenuator has reduced variety **below the threshold** of the required response.

We say that the responding system does not exhibit

REQUISITE VARIETY

— a most important notion to which we must often return.

Thus the most obvious recourse in both cases is to reduce the degree of attenuation recently notified. The works' manager will want to register the class of information, not so far registered, that is causing labour problems. The marketing manager will want to respond to the expected demand of fourteen colours.

But suppose that the operation really **cannot** (as originally postulated) accommodate the necessary stocks. And suppose the works' manager is simply forbidden to acknowledge the nauseous combination of orders (because of possible legal consequences).

What about the question mark now?

This is for certain: you cannot repeal

THE LAW OF REQUISITE VARIETY

— which says that **only variety can absorb variety**.

LOW VARIETY is necessarily enhanced, or amplified, to the number of possible states that the receiving entity needs if it is to remain regulated.

So we mark the low-variety input on a diagram with the (electrician's) symbol for an

(which is a triangle simply, and not a directional arrow). This completes our repertoire of balancing actions (remember *homeostasis* again).

Here then is the completed diagram on which we have been working:

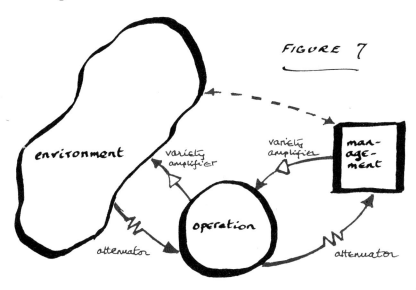

The dotted line comes in for the sake of completeness. It will be discussed later. For the moment, the management's interest in the environment is mediated by the actual operations that it undertakes there (for in reality the operation is embedded in the environment, and the management in *it*).

Evidently the two variety amplifiers have been invoked to proffer solutions to the two residual problems.

THEN DO THIS NEXT:

Specify how you would use the variety amplifiers to restore **requisite variety**, and thereby to create acceptable conditions for **homeostatic regulation**.

NOTE: We are not yet discussing the collection of DATA or the flow of INFORMATION. This is about the FUNCTIONS that are competent to engineer with variety.

ANSWERS

The works' manager may enrich the structure of the payment system. He increases its variety to accommodate, through greater flexibility in calculating rewards, the problems that he must dissolve — without specific acknowledgement of the suppressed causes. The employment, in short, rewards higher variety.

The marketing manager needs to 'increase' the variety of eleven to a variety of fourteen without an increase in stock. One way is to decouple the production line through intermediate stocks (so that one unpainted pot may be painted *either* red or blue). Another way is by advertising — that potent variety amplifier. A 'special offer' can be formulated; a projection implying more colours than are actually available can be mounted.

The reason why Figure 7 did not adhere solely to amplification, considering this separately (as Figure 6 separately considered attenuation), should be emerging in the head of anyone really working on these exercises. We are dealing with **continuous loops** of variety involvement, not with isolated bits of apparatus.

Hence emphasis has been placed on homeostasis. We are seeking balance through requisite variety.

Therefore:

- many management strategies are *mixed* between adjustments to amplifiers and attenuators

    (indeed, it is often a matter of choice as to whether a specific contingency is viewed as one or the other, carrying a different sign — plus or minus)

    — we need only to be satisfied that as the dynamic interaction between entities unfolds, we have made provision that no entity will be swamped — inevitably out of control — by the proliferation of another's variety.

- In view of this, the problem of measurement is minimal. We shall not find ourselves *counting* the number of possible states, but looking for assurances that counter-balanced varieties are roughly equal.

    To take a vivid and omnipresent example: The human brain has *about* ten thousand million neurons — nerve cells — in it, and these are capable of generating who knows how many patterns. The variety is legion. But whatever it is, another human brain roughly matches the first's variety. Thus if two people, who have put in exactly the same number of hours' practice, sit down to play chess, we would be wise to bet evens on the outcome — and without counting the neurons first.

- The problem of management itself, which is that of regulating an immense proliferation of variety, is less horrific once the underlying homeostatic regulators are perceived, properly designed, and allowed to absorb the variety of each others' entities.

    This is the essence of VIABILITY.

These explorations should make the following formal statement readily accessible:

The First Principle of Organization

Managerial, operational and environmental varieties,
diffusing through an institutional system,
TEND TO EQUATE;
*they should be **designed** to do so with minimum damage to*
people and to cost.

If this Principle is indeed accessible, it is by no means orthodox — and we have made a breakthrough in our managerial outlook. For what the Principle is saying is that viable systems, and these include giant corporations, are basically *self*-organizing. If it were not so, then the management would be totally overwhelmed by the variety proliferated (as we say) 'lower down'.

But variety absorbs variety, and systems run to homeostasis, because all the subsystems are inter-connected — as we have begun to see — and complexities cancel each other out. Variety is soaked up on a football field by a redshirt marking a whiteshirt *and* vice-versa. The product 'marks' its market, and the market 'marks' its product.

By the same token, in proliferation of variety terms, management 'marks' its operation, and vice-versa. Let's be clear: at a management meeting called to scrutinize operational results, the operations people will have managerial attitudes under equivalent scrutiny. Then ideas that would be rejected tend not to be advanced; and happenings that are disapproved tend not to have happened at all — that is (I have been there) they somehow don't show up in the records. In such a meeting there has to be enormous variety attenuation — otherwise, by the Law of Requisite Variety, we should operate our businesses only in alternate weeks, and conduct enquiries into the operations in the weeks that alternate.

Here are two points relating to this:

- Management MEETINGS are excellent examples of homeostasis in high-variety situations:

  > the meeting will end in due course with some show of agreement;
  > whether the meeting has been productive or not will depend on how variety has been absorbed.

  Because the situation has high variety, heavy attenuators must be in use — notably an agreed low-variety model of the situation (standard reports, and so on).

  Thereafter, the **design** of the meeting

  > — agenda, protocol, rubrics — all variety reducers —

  is crucial to a productive outcome.

- The function of management is emerging, as it must finally be understood, as a subsystem of the viable system — and not as some hierarchic overlord.

  All five subsystems to be encountered in the VSM have their own languages, their own criteria, their own figures-of-speech — and their own satisfactions.

  Management is one such subsystem, and System One is another. They, with the remaining three, are **mutually interdependent**.

is *this* point, then, properly made?

If all subsystems are *vital to viability*, then there is no meaning to 'more important'.

> That managers 'give themselves airs' is merely a public notification of their subsystemic role, like carrying a business card. The good ones, as you would expect, know this.

Perhaps we have chattered enough to bring these notions home, although it must take time and also exercise to become familiar with what may well be a wholly novel approach. But this can hardly be postponed any longer:

RETRIEVE YOUR LIST

of the embedded subsidiaries or departments that between them produce the company (or whatever else may be your System-in-focus).

— This list adds up to SYSTEM ONE.

MAKE A LARGE DIAGRAM —
ONE FOR EACH OF THEM —
TO LOOK LIKE FIGURE 7.

It is a good idea to omit the red captions (you know what the symbols mean), and to create enough space

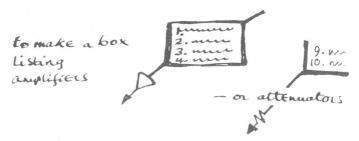

to make a box listing amplifiers

— or attenuators

WRITE IN

all the mechanisms that pertain to variety engineering in pursuit of homeostasis, and in recollection of the Law of Requisite Variety.

Nothing of any importance should be left out of these diagrams. For example, the market has been mentioned as part of the environment for a manufacturing company. But so is the 'ecology' of raw material supply (how is *that* attenuated?) So is the social climate a part. You may wish to divide the environment into sections, and give each **separately** a box of amplifiers and attenuators to connect it to the operation.

BE CREATIVE WITH THESE NEW TOOLS!

By way of refreshment before beginning this task, consider how varieties come to equate in a public service organization with which everyone is familiar . . .

The police force exercises two main functions. One is to protect the citizen from law-breakers, and the other is to prevent the citizen from breaking the law himself.

Since no individual citizen can do more than one of these things at a time, one policeman could undertake to safeguard him and also to thwart his misdemeanours. They would sleep and eat at the same time!

This arrangement would provide Requisite Variety, but it is not practicable. However, as soon as you give one policeman two citizens to watch, one of them may commit a robbery or get mugged while the other is under observation. Hence crime, given or received.

It turns out that in fact Britain has about five hundred citizens for every policeman. It follows that to do their job the police need to amplify their ordinary human capacities by 500 times. Note the built-in assumption: *What is it?* ✳

To this end the police amplify their variety — with guns, certainly, but more routinely by using fast cars and radio. Computers and systems of informers are best regarded, perhaps, as attenuators of incoming variety: they reduce the number of possible states of suspicion by eliminating suspects.

It is good practice to examine familiar systems in terms of variety, and interesting thoughts may be provoked. Here are a couple or three:

- How is expenditure divided between amplifying protection, amplifying prevention?
  How does the trade-off between them actually work?

  E.g.: alarm systems
       versus pursuit

✳ The assumption is that the prison population is stable.

- What are the trade-offs where technology is concerned?

    E.g.: cars get around more with fewer men;
        men get around less with far more penetration of the
        public scene.

    E.g.: do you spend money on the sense-organs — tapping
        information at source or on the 'central nervous system'
        — computers and data-banks.

- Why all of this about **police amplification** when homeostasis
  may also be reached through **attenuation of public variety**?

  That is, preventative laws ('no access', curfews, identity
  papers) which restrict societary states imply less police
  amplification — because monitoring is a lower variety activity
  than coping with the unexpected.

  How does this bear on freedom?

      — is the second means of obtaining requisite variety
      actually any more alarming than the first (just because
      the connotations are unsavoury)?

MAKE A PRACTICE

of experimenting (mentally, and on a scribbling pad) with
the new concepts being disclosed here as they are
exemplified in systems (such as the police force) with the
functions, problems and shortcomings of which any citizen
is familiar.

Listen to public debates in the media with these cybernetic
considerations in mind. How much of what you then hear
and see becomes fatuous?

SPECIAL TERMS OF § TWO

VARIETY   a measure of complexity: the number of possible states of a system.

THE LAW OF   only variety can absorb variety
REQUISITE   (Ashby's Law)
VARIETY

ATTENUATOR   a device that reduces variety, depicted thus:

AMPLIFIER   a device that increases variety, depicted thus:

THE FIRST PRINCIPLE OF ORGANIZATION

Managerial, operational and environmental varieties, diffusing through an institutional system, tend to equate;

they should be **designed** to do so with minimal damage to people and to cost.

§ THREE

Right at the start (look at Figure 1) the convention was established that all the elements of System One depend from a Senior Management box. Figure 1 seems to imply that the second also depends from the first, the third from the second, and so on. Not so: the central line, which might be called the 'command axis', is taken to interact with each subsidiary management box independently.

Moreover, what appears in Figure 1 as a single line will obviously constitute a whole cable of separate threads.

The next job is to start considering what those threads represent.

I You should have your System One diagrams beside you, and think about each case, as the (inevitably) more general discussion unfolds.

First of all —

GRASP THIS NETTLE:

The management of the System-in-focus, called the Senior Management, is IN PRINCIPLE unable to entertain the variety generated by any one (never mind all) of its subsidiary viable systems that constitute System One.

The beginnings of a theory of autonomy, of de-centralization, lie in this simple fact —

rather than in political theory. It is a 'nettle to grasp', because the senior management often assumes — and likes to exercise — the power to poke around in the intimate managerial detail of its subsidiaries in System One.

But THINK: the so-called prerogative to intervene indiscriminately

does not have Requisite Variety.

It cannot be competently done.

It can be done in the sense that a bully can do what he likes: pulling guns or pulling rank is an amplifier of one's undoubted authority, and an attenuator of the subservient creature's own variety. But the homeostasis that results is momentary, and hence incompetent.

In a modern organization, the fundamental variety balancers are those shown in the diagram facing:-

Legal and Corporate Requirements are those variety attenuators that signify the identity of subsidiaries as corporate entities. Legally, System One is bound into the parent System-in-focus by its Articles of Association, and by all the provisions of the Companies' Act that concern affiliation. But the parent may, and usually does, specify other constraints on the proliferation of System One's variety. These range from delimiting technologies to specifying the modus operandi.

VERY WELL:

List them for each of your embedded System One elements.

The Resource Bargain is the 'deal' by which some degree of autonomy is agreed between the Senior Management and its junior counterparts.

The bargain declares: out of all the activities that System One elements might undertake, THESE will be

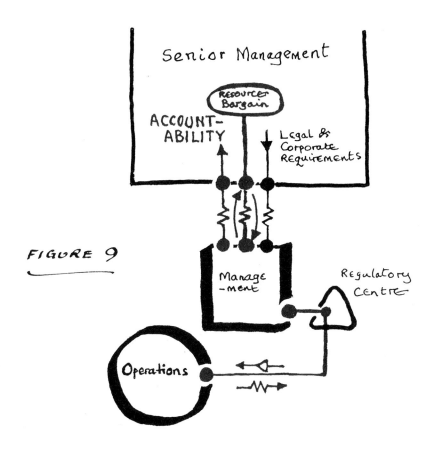

FIGURE 9

tackled (and not *those*), and the resources negotiated to these ends will be provided.

The homeostatic loop sketched into the diagram properly indicates that a **dynamic process** is involved. It is essentially attenuative, because it excludes a huge range of alternatives. This is not to say that the senior management never provides variety amplification to the junior enterprise within the attenuating scheme: it may, by superior knowledge or through unexpected financing, open up opportunities not conceived by System One on its own initiative.

> **NOW LIST** your mechanisms for striking the Resource Bargain for each subsidiary.

NOTE: Should it turn out that all that happens in reality is that the Boss says: **Do This**, or **These are your norms**, then you still have a resource bargain by uniliteral edict. But planning ought to be a continuous process whereby things are done now — explicitly, resources are committed — so that the future may be different.

Note on this Note:
INVESTMENT IS A VARIETY ATTENUATOR.

In any case, and however autocratic or democratic (or even anarchic) your Resource Bargaining proves to be, the governing mode of management is

Accountability. Please think about this *responsibility for resources provided* in terms (not of financial probity, not of emotional dependency, but) of variety engineering.

Can you possibly itemize every single thing that the subsidiary does, demand a report on it, and expect a justification? Obviously not. Therefore accountability is an **attentuation** of high-variety happenings.

NOW EXAMINE precisely how accountability is exercised, and especially what attenuators (totals, averages, key indicators . . .) are used. Summarize the findings.

If in the end, you are appalled to discover that the machinery is inadequate, that Senior Management just does not have Requisite Variety, then you had better own up. Your System-in-focus has a System One that simply is **not accountable**.

Evidently something must urgently be done. But there is no need to panic: yours is the usual case.
People spend small fortunes on systems analysis, computers, and so on, but they don't understand the Law of Requisite Variety. The effort avails them nothing.

Every management team has some sort of office attached to it, but Figure 9 dignifies its activity (and with good reason) by calling it a

Regulatory Centre.

Management in System One is charged with conducting its operations according to a Resource Bargain struck with Senior Management. Then the transmission of plans, programmes and procedures to the operational circle should be regarded as an act of *regulation*.

This regulation, as the diagram shows, amplifies managerial variety: the basic details of the Resource Bargain must be elaborated. This regulation also attenuates operational variety: operational potentiality must be harnessed to agreed objectives. Thus the Regulatory Centre (the activities of which are marked diagrammatically by a triangle) is the focus of homeostasis between management and operations.

NOW DO THIS:

Make a list of regulatory actions that mediate between System One managements and their operations.

These exist in one *locus of homeostasis* for analytical purposes: where are their physical locations? Perhaps you remembered the production control office, and forgot the Boss's outer office — where his secretary is the most effective variety manipulator in the set-up.

There is a question as to whether all the regulatory actions, in their various locations, actually cohere in providing Requisite Variety — and therefore whether the locus of homeosatasis ought to be more than a logical concept of the Regulatory Centre, marked by a triangle. Perhaps it should have a more physical embodiment, as an organizational entity . . .?

41

This shift in emphasis from manipulations of variety in principle to their embodiment in physical form is a transition worth comment — because people often confuse the two modes of management. Explicitly:

- What *strategies* offer Requisite Variety?
      — remember the discussions around Figure 7 about marketable colours and about wage structures;
- What *channels* are in place to contain the variety of information flow, and of data transmission?

Both aspects of variety handling demand the satisfaction of the Law of Requisite Variety.

EXAMPLES:

- A library contains (guaranteed!) all the knowledge there is about bees. Then it has in principle Requisite Variety to handle all my bee-keeping queries.

   After joining the library, I discover that every one of the books is stored only in its Chinese version. It has zero channel capacity to transmit to me the adequate variety it houses.

- Rushing to the library next door, in which all information is stored in English, thereby assuring me that the channel matches my English-speaking variety, I join.

   But the storehouse itself does not have Requisite Variety: there is not a single item under 'bees' in the whole index.

NO USE to have flexible policies capable of generating hundreds of product variations, if the computer *format* allows only one-digit discrimination between products.

NO USE providing enough bits in the computer to differentiate every person in the world, if your *strategy* is to market in your own country alone.

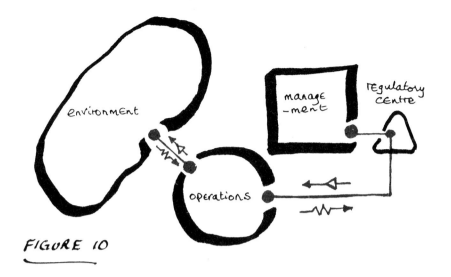

FIGURE 10

This new figure, then, is devoted in the first place to finding the balance of Requisite Variety in the **channels** used to transmit variety already understood to be provided in policy terms (cf Figure 7).

INSTANCES on the operational loop:

- a Resource Bargain that 'knows' we can make 1000 units this month has to be _amplified_ into a _production schedule_ providing Requisite Variety: i.e. exactly what each machine has to do shift by shift.

- operational activity that includes every kind of happenstance, from broken bolts to streaming colds, from lightning strikes to power failures, has to be monitored under variety _attenuation_ in a _reporting_ system.

In both cases, the channels must convey **more than** the variety of the schedules and reports concerned, to allow for a little redundancy.

Without a little redundancy (day _plus_ date, machine number _plus_ name, figures _plus_ words, and so on) ambiguities will appear (due to omissions, bad writing, mistakes, and so on) that cannot be resolved.

43

INSTANCES on the environmental loop:

- a product strategy offers requisite variety in principle, but it has to be *amplified* towards the market in practice through channels carrying
  — products, i.e. the distribution system
  — information, i.e. advertising, premiums, offers
  ALSO in requisite variety.

- the environment includes
  — suppliers, whose channels are their (amplifying) catalogues, between which an *attenuating* protocol must be established
  — customers, whose channels are depletion of inventory (i.e. they purchase things) notified, return of guarantees with market-segment data attached, letters of complaint, and market research itself: all *attenuating* a notionally infinite variety.

Again, the question is no longer whether all these activities can **generate** Requisite Variety (as to which we assured ourselves earlier), but whether there is channel capacity adequate to the data flows involved.

For example, do you *know* how much information can be transferred through the channel of a magazine advertisement chanced upon, or through a roadside bill-board glanced upon?

NOW DO THIS:

Make lists of your own instances relating to the two-way channels between management/operations and operations/environment.

CHANNEL capacity for TRANSMITTING VARIETY is the discussion point — not (as before) the generation of variety, strategically, as a source.

What **measures** do you have — or need?

44

Now that we have sufficiently clearly distinguished between Requisite Variety as manifested in the three entitites of the diagram, and Requisite Variety as available channel capacity, by experiment as well as by definition, we should formalize

The Second Principle of Organization

The four directional channels carrying information between the management unit, the operation, and the environment must each have a higher capacity to transmit a given amount of information relevant to variety selection in a given time than the originating subsystem has to generate it in that time.

The second Principle invokes a *time base*, which the first Principle did not (except to speak of a tendency on which no limits are placed). This is because the capacity of an actual channel depends absolutely on the rate of data transmission involved. Note also that *data* are transmitted, not variety itself. Variety is amplified or attenuated by the instructions that the data formulate; but those instructions must be adequate to the relevant variety selection.

EXAMPLE:

We may seek to modify a customer's behaviour (from not-buying to buying), a variety of two, by writing him a letter.

The letter says: 'Dear customer . . . advantages . . . now BUY'. The variety matches. The channel capacity required is also two (make, or not, a photocopy to all customers: the Post Office takes care of the increased variety in channels once the batch of say 1000 letters is mailed). The addressing machine automatically serializes the addresses.

If we now personalize each letter, taking account of special knowledge about each customer, we shall need a channel capable of generating a thousand letters, instead of one, in the time available.

It should instantly have occurred to you that whether the provision of this channel capacity is difficult or not depends almost entirely on the technology in use.

If each of a thousand letters involves data handling by a desk researcher's consulting a manilla folder and putting together appropriate paragraphs (even if each of these is stereotyped), and a typist is then needed to type out the result, then the channelling of all this selection of states that underwrites the variety deployed according to the First Principle will be a major undertaking. Speaking of rates, it might take ten days at a hundred letters a day. But of course the whole job could be done in an hour or two inside a computerised system.

In drawing up lists of amplifiers and attenuators, then, and in seeking to evaluate homeostatic variety balances, we should consider that VARIETY GENERATORS may have to be dealt with, or may be designed to absorb naturally proliferating variety. If we look on technology as such a variety generator, and not simply as a producer of artefacts, then our regulatory capability is enhanced — as well as our ability to undertake novel things, or to run processes more economically.

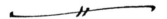

Considering that our recursive modelling procedure does not permit us to investigate the infrastructure of our three entities without changing the System-in-focus, quite a lot of managerially powerful conclusions are emerging. By treating the environment, the operations, and the management unit simply as 'black boxes', that is as opaque to analysis, and looking only at their interactions, we have been able to enunciate two Principles of Organization — and to draw up an accounting of varietal interactions that conduce to homeostasis. If these listings have been conscientiously made, and the relevant amplifiers, attenuators, and technological generators considered in terms of Requisite Varieties, some telling discoveries about the viable system under study may have been made already.

But we have not finished with System One, even now.

The diagrammatic conventions are powerful. Even though our boxes are 'empty', and our channels merely lines, there has been much to say: but are the conventions thereby exhausted? No. There are big red blobs on all the figures, and they have a special meaning.

TRANSDUCTION is the word we need: 'leading across'. Each red blob is a *transducer*, and it has this function:

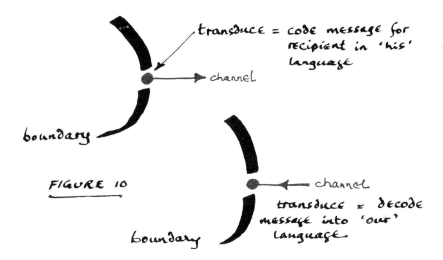

transduce = code message for recipient in 'his' language

channel

boundary

FIGURE 10

channel

transduce = decode message into 'our' language

boundary

The Third Principle of Organization

Wherever the information carried on a channel capable of distinguishing a given variety crosses a boundary, it undergoes transduction; the variety of the transducer must be at least equivalent to the variety of the channel.

It is self-evident — once pointed out!

The point is to draw a clear distinction between channel capacity and transduction capacity: they are not at all the same thing. People think too loosely about 'communicating the message', as if any sort of connexion must be able to do the job.

EXAMPLES:

There are eight transducers in our basic diagram. These
examples are all *actual cases* of inadequate variety in
transduction — **given that** basic variety (First Principle) is
capable of absorption, and channel capacity (Second Principle)
can convey that variety.

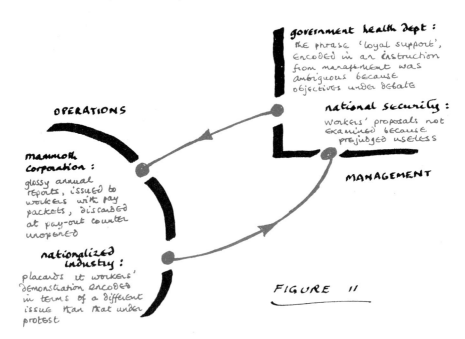

government health dept:
The phrase 'loyal support',
encoded in an instruction
from management was
ambiguous because
objectives under debate

national security:
workers' proposals not
examined because
prejudged useless

OPERATIONS

MANAGEMENT

mammoth corporation:
glossy annual
reports, issued to
workers with pay
packets, discarded
at pay-out counter
unopened

nationalized industry:
placards it workers'
demonstration encoded
in terms of a different
issue than that under
protest

FIGURE 11

Note: Because these examples concern only the *transduction* of
messages, the question whether the message itself intends to
amplify or to attenuate variety is irrelevant. The job of the
transducer is to **preserve** variety, whatever it is.

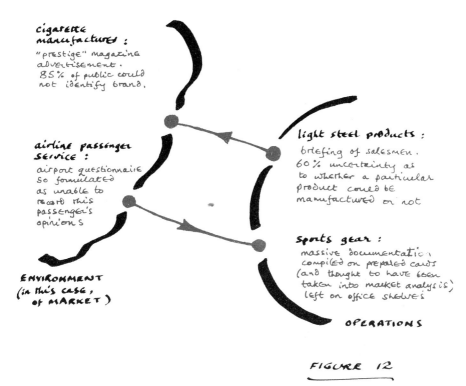

cigarette
manufacturers :
"prestige" magazine
advertisement.
85% of public could
not identify brand.

airline passenger
service :
airport questionnaire
so formulated
as unable to
record this
passenger's
opinions

light steel products :
briefing of salesmen.
60% uncertainty as
to whether a particular
product could be
manufactured or not

sports gear :
massive documentation
compiled on prepared cards
(and thought to have been
taken into market analysis)
left on office shelves

ENVIRONMENT
(in this case,
of MARKET)

OPERATIONS

FIGURE 12

Taking these case examples as guides:

NOW DO THIS:

Make similar analytic vignettes of the transducers that
populate your own System One . . .

. . . don't forget that you have more than one diagram
to consider!

— AND TRY TO MAKE
an enormous diagram of the double-loop (management
⮂ operations ⮂ environment) for each one,
annotating for the **THREE PRINCIPLES**.

The whole collection of diagrams is now put together in a particular composite of very special significance.

(All other aspects of our work are *implicit* in this Figure. The Law of Requisite Variety bids us to be *selective*.)

Here it is:

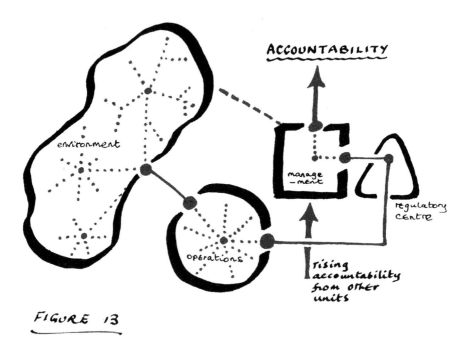

FIGURE 13

The star-like *networks* are collecting information which has very high variety, and must necessarily be attenuated by the management strategies designed to procure homeostasis (First Principle).

The *channels* are variety-adequate to convey the data that select this Requisite Variety (Second Principle).

The *transducers* on the **horizontal axis**, which have just been discussed, use coding mechanisms (Third Principle).

In ACCOUNTABILITY we meet our first transducer on the **vertical axis** (compare Figure 9).

This 'leads across' the boundary between System One and the Senior Management — and of course it involves massive variety attenuation.

Precisely:

- Each System One must attenuate its horizontal variety —
    that whereby its operations are made effective within
    its environment
  in order to discharge its Resource Bargain with the Senior Management.

- This Bargain is concerned with the *homeostasis of resourcefulness*. Then accountability would, in a perfectly designed system, consist simply in transmitting a continuous signal — a monotonous tone — meaning 'everything proceeds as agreed'.

- Senior Managements are unlikely to accept that so great a variety attenuation (notifying only two possible states, OK or not-OK) is Requisite in their terms. But the *maximum* variety they can handle for each subsidiary is their own total capacity divided by the number of subsidiaries in System One.

THEREFORE:

The design of accountability transducers and channels must conform to the variety attenuation already built in to the managerial strategy —
    that is: the Second and Third Principles can be interpreted
    only in terms of the First.

AND:

Senior Management, having agreed to this designed accountability (and subject to safeguards to be discussed later), must not often exercise its prerogative to conduct star-chamber investigations — or confidence will be forfeit and autonomy denatured. In particular, it has no access to the subsidiary's Regulatory Centre — which is the local management's service domain.

51

Finally, and in preparation for the next section (in which System One will be synthesized), please look again at Figure 9 — and the surrounding discussion of the Resource Bargain.

The bargain itself constitutes a massive variety attenuator: it is a dynamic process whereby all the states that the elemental System One might adopt are chopped down to the programme it is agreed to undertake.

AFTER this (essentially *planning*) process is complete, then routine management must set up a routine interaction whereby the Resource Bargain is implemented.

Now no-one is going to arrive on Monday mornings with a sackful of gold, saying: 'here are your resources, bring me the change on Saturday:

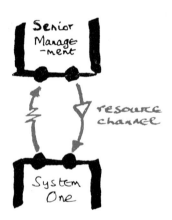

an ACCOUNTABILITY LOOP —

which is drawn here specially to emphasize that it is a *regular homeostat*

— we are used to looking at it horizontally.

All the Principles of Organization apply to this loop.

The RESOURCE CHANNEL transmits **permissions** essentially, and needs amplifiers to explain their operation. The accountability return loop attenuates the whole continuous saga of life in System One into **requisite** variety.

These remarks concern the SECOND Principle.

REFLECT NOW on **all three** Principles as exemplified in this sketch, and as they apply in your own System-in-focus.

52

SPECIAL TERMS OF § THREE

CHANNEL CAPACITY   *a measure of the amount of information*
                                      that can be transmitted in a given amount
                                      of time

TRANSDUCER   *encodes or decodes a message whenever*
   ('leading across')   *it crosses a system boundary — and*
                                        therefore needs a different mode of
                                        expression.

THE SECOND PRINCIPLE OF ORGANIZATION

The four directional channels carrying information between the management unit, the operation, and the environment must each have a higher capacity to transmit a given amount of information relevant to variety selection in a given time than the originating subsystem has to generate it in that time.

(Relies on Shannon's Tenth Theorem)

THE THIRD PRINCIPLE OF ORGANIZATION

Wherever the information carried on a channel capable of distinguishing a given variety crosses a boundary, it undergoes transduction; the variety of the transducer must be at least equivalent to the variety of the channel.

§ FOUR

With the enunciation of three organizational principles, we have at last exhausted the spatial potentialities of the basic diagram that depicts an element of System One, an element that is itself a viable system.

However, we have not said much about time. The temporal context is obvious enough; we acknowledge it by speaking about *tendency* in the First Principle, *trans*duction (which is also a temporal process) in the Third, but above all in the Second Principle where *rates* of data transmission actually define capacity in a channel. Standing back to observe the whole of this system in action, however, we can see that we face more than a spatial system in a temporal context: it is a dynamic process. Here is a group of variety generators in continuous production of systemic states, so **organized** (by the Three Principles) as to absorb each other's proliferation of variety. Then part of this organization must have to do with the dynamo itself, and we add:

The Fourth Principle of Organization

The operation of the first three principles must be cyclically maintained through time without hiatus or lags.

Why was not this Principle included with the others to conclude the last section? In fact, and although each elemental viable system has its own dynamic on the horizontal axis (wherein its local management enjoys autonomy), the general dynamics of the System-in-focus derive from the *vertical* axis, which we are only now ready to examine fully.

Please turn the page.

Figure 14 gives a complete structural account of System One: the total collection of embedded viable systems that comprises the next lower recursion of the System-in-focus. Of course, the diagrammatic convention is meant to invoke all that has so far been learnt about these four (arbitrarily four) systems displayed on the horizontal axis.

● Remember: There is no significance in the fact that they make a kind of list, in which one system appears to have 'higher rank' than another.

● Remember also: The vertical 'command' axis, now reduced diagrammatically to three channels, in 'passing through' all the management boxes is assumed to have independent access to each. The channels shown are the resources-being-applied (according to various rules and programmes), and the continuous accountability for them, which between them form a homeostatic loop, and the intervention channel — which issues legal and other corporate commands. This second input to System One may also be regarded as a loop, closed this time by mere obedience.

NOW DO THIS:

Take a large sheet of paper, and begin designing your own Figure 14 for your own System-in-focus like this:

draw for a start ONLY the operational circles of the elements you have already isolated and examined separately, and think about the connexions between them.

These connexions are depicted by the squiggly red lines in the picture shown ⟶

Here are some tips:

(i) about the circles themselves —

● what is their relative importance,

● by what most informative measure?

- then consider varying their size as a way of **communicating** this information.

The eye sees *area*, not radius. So if turnover (for example) is the area = πr^2, divide the turnover by (oh, roughly) 3, and take the square root for the circle's radius.

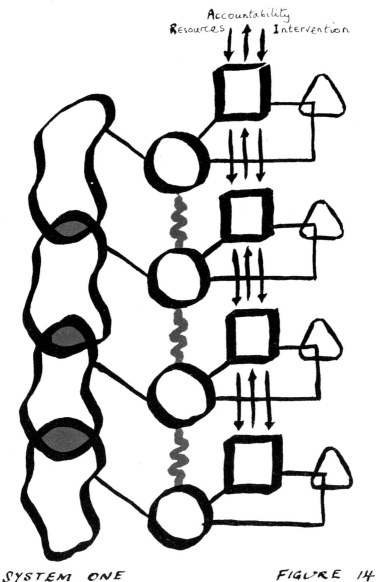

SYSTEM ONE   FIGURE 14

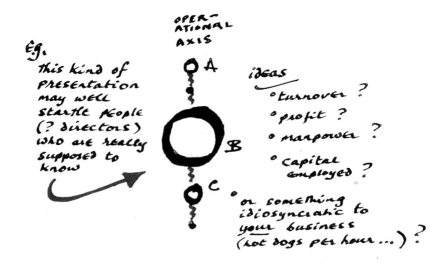

OPER-
ATIONAL
AXIS

Eg.
this kind of
presentation
may well
startle people
(? directors)
who are really
supposed to
know

ideas
∘ turnover ?
∘ profit ?
∘ manpower ?
∘ capital
   employed ?

∘ or something
idiosyncratic to
your business
(hot dogs per hour ...) ?

- if nothing worth COMMUNICATING is to be gained from this approach — don't use it. Leave the circles uniform, and emphasize something else in the diagram.

   (Requisite Variety for your readers, after all . . .)

(ii) about the connecting squiggly lines —

- the basic convention on the operational axis is the same as that on the command axis. That is, the simple arrangement shown in Figure 14 does not mean that the operations flow serially into each other: only that there *are* connexions . . .

- for instance, operations may be so loosely coupled (e.g. in a conglomerate) that the connexion is no more than a competition for capital. In such cases, the conventions of Figure 14 are adequate (we shall see how adequate later).

- Sometimes operations are very strongly connected, and indeed do flow into each other. In such cases, arrange the operations in the appropriate order — and enhance the squiggly lines
   (this puts into empirical effect the discussion of Figure 2)
- or matters may be yet more complicated

IN SHORT:

Always be as creative as possible. A VSM diagram that looks exactly like a stereotype from one of the books about the VSM cannot possibly be exploiting the model.

HOWEVER:

Keep to the diagrammatic conventions themselves: fundamental blocs and connectivities — as also the horizontal and vertical axes — have been found to be powerful in analysis and diagnosis.

ESPECIALLY:

Ensure that modified diagrams do not flout the axioms, principles and laws of the Viable System expounded here — which they are meant precisely to illustrate.

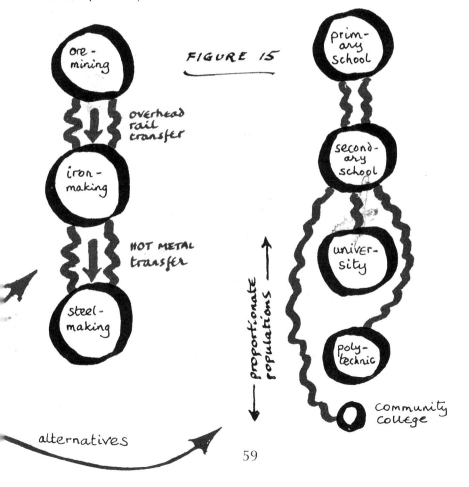

FIGURE 15

Assuming that a suitable depiction of the vertical operational axis has been drawn (and suitably annotated), consider the environments.

Figure 14 again shows the basic convention:

- each elemental viable system has its own uniquely defined environment —

which however intersects with *all* the others } at the very least, the organization's name is shared in the public mind. * *see below*

although the convention (Figure 14, red intersects) joins only neighbouring environments.

Any feasible combination of environments is acceptable. It is possible moreover to make very creative use of this diagrammatic space — which houses all the variety generators with which the System-in-focus has to deal — by including in it subsystems and transducers that you have analysed empirically 'in the field'.

Here are the **two limiting cases**:

- the environments of all the subsystems (elements) of System One are identical.
  Then all operational circles are connected to one and the same environmental envelope.
  > e.g.: a supermarket
  > — whose departments are all supplied by one corporate wholesaler,
  > — whose customers for all departments indiscriminately are the local population.

- the environments of all the subsystems (elements) of System One are *geographically* separate.
  > e.g. a country
  > — whose provinces are run by local governments.
  > The diagram facing, Figure 16, shows how to depict environments where the intersections are minimal, but in this case
  > Canadian, Canada-ness, Canada-hood, the Maple-Leaf-for-ever.

* *an Example*

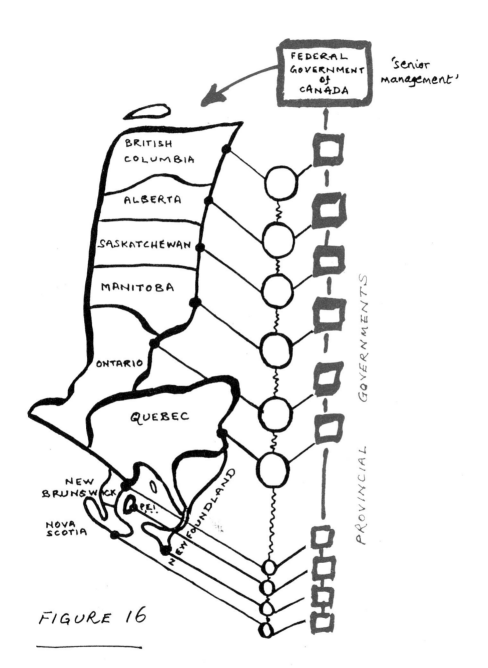

FEDERAL GOVERNMENT of CANADA

'senior management'

BRITISH COLUMBIA

ALBERTA

SASKATCHEWAN

MANITOBA

ONTARIO

QUEBEC

NEW BRUNSWICK

P.E.I.

NOVA SCOTIA

NEWFOUNDLAND

PROVINCIAL GOVERNMENTS

FIGURE 16

In Figure 16 we see how to begin sketching the Big Diagram with which we hope to finish.

PRACTICAL NOTE:
It will prove very difficult to display everything that is important on a single sheet of paper, however large (and this makes these explanations even more difficult on these small sheets). Then decisions must be taken as to how to break up the total account.

For instance, Figure 16 exemplifies such a decision. I wanted to emphasize the handling of the environmental picture — and so we have quite a respectable map of Canada. But because this is more-or-less proportionate, there is no space in which to 'make points' with graphics on the operational axis. The economically underprivileged Maritime Provinces have smaller circles — but so what?

But if the environmental 'map' can be expanded to (say) 6 feet high, then the circles can be made proportional to the 'GNP' of the Provinces. Try to visualize how bloated wealthy Ontario and British Columbia then look! When I displayed a VSM based on this graphic device in government circles in Ottawa — to top civil servants who *knew* the facts — there were gasps of amazement all round.

Similarly, I have often presented management groups with wall charts of only bits of the VSM's subsystems (that conveyed all the details of important homeostatic loops for example), or had them poring over a ten-foot chart of environmental subsystems.

It is for you to decide how to present the Big Diagram when the work is all done.

- It is at the moment my task to decide how to present the Big Diagram to YOU.

    THESE TASKS ARE DIFFERENT.

    ⋆ You know what the System-in-focus actually **is** (I have to generalize and exemplify).

★ You have lots of space — USE IT. Make visual presentations, rather than write reports.

NOW DO THIS:

Look again at Figure 14.

Look at the drawings you made of your own OPERATIONAL AXIS — the last exercise.

DRAW YOUR OWN FIGURE 14
— making appropriate environmental conventions to fit the operational ones (which you might now decide to alter)
— completing the managerial box-and-triangle structures.

NOTE: You must decide in particular how much detail about the double-homeostats to show: that is, your deployment of the Principles of Organization in the handling of variety — horizontally.

Whether you end up with a single large sheet of paper, or a summary sheet with detailed Appendices, you should at this point be able to say with satisfaction:

'**THIS** is my full account of System One'. Done. ✓

Now we come to a new topic with its own new concept. It is a specific sickness of homeostasis that we need to understand.

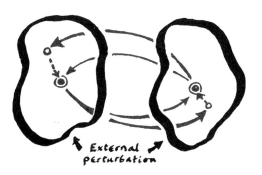

External perturbation

Take this diagram to represent a homeostat.

The bull's eye ◉ stands for the stable state of each subsystem. So the inner red loop stands for the stability of the whole.

When the stable point wanders *o*, it is *drawn back* to ◉.

All that looks very peaceful. Close inspection suggests why: the relationship is somewhat incestuous. The system is closed.

The system we are studying is not at all closed. In Figure 17 (facing) we see a version of the familiar System One. All the usual conventions apply; but we shall now concern ourselves with the elemental subsystem B — surrounded, as you see, by A on the one side and C on the other.

- B has a role on the horizontal axis. The B management has a duty to conduct B operations in the B environment
    as effectively as possible.
  What are the constraints on this endeavour?

  B MUST

      (i) obey the dictates (few, we trust) of the corporate intervention,

      (ii) operate within the terms of the Resource Bargain,

      (iii) acknowledge the squiggly-line relationships (strong or weak) with the operations of A and C,

and   (iv) note whatever environmental intersects impinge on freedom of action as to advertizing for instance.

  But B, despite these four vertical squeezes still has all his managerial virility . . . off he goes.

- The B management mounts his operations in the B circle. These repercuss along the squiggly lines, and (because of B's ignorance of A and C operations, of whose *total* variety he is *inevitably* ignorant) they have explosive impacts ⚡ . The operations then produce their intended effects in the B environment. And again, there are powerful reverberations in both the A and C environments . ⚡ . . .

- What are the A and C managements to make of these explosions? Upsets in both their environments and their own operations are channeled back — and obviously they address their colleague B management in outspoken ⚡ terms.

64

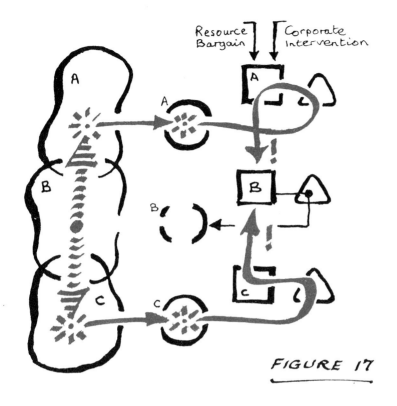

FIGURE 17

- B is a good colleague, and a loyal member of the enterprise. He tries to take these complaints into account.

BUT

  - Meanwhile,
    THE SAME THING is happening to A (who is being assailed by B and (say) Z) and to C (in the face of complaints from B and D).

IN SHORT

Because *every* element is continuously trying to adjust to every element, **nothing ever settles down**.

The sickness of the homeostat is:
    OSCILLATION.

And the cure for the sickness:
    OSCILLATION must be DAMPED.

Of course, in practice these events do not take place in the ordered sequence used here for expository reasons — someone would intervene (one hopes) and call a conference to resolve matters. The point is that all these influences are 'in there pitching', and that we can penetrate all the oscillatory confusion to understand (no, not 'the cause') that it has to be damped. Moreover, if we look back to Figure 14, we can see by a graphical clue that the right-hand side of the diagram has all its horizontal elements floating in space: those triangles obviously need anchoring somehow.

> Yes, I craftily drew it like that to bring home the point. It seems to be necessary; otherwise the United States and the Soviet Union would see why armament policies oscillate, and (as we expected of the folk in the previous two pages) would do something about it.

The fact is that **System Two** —

the viable system's anti-oscillatory device for System One

is almost totally misunderstood and under-represented in contemporary management technique. It is always present, or the organization would shake itself to pieces. But because it is not properly handled, enterprises **come very close** to disintegration:

- like the East—West detente,
- like the North—South economic equilibrium,
- like the Public Service Borrowing Requirement's homeostasis,
- like the budget for health or education,
- like the Company's cash-flow stability,
- like the capital locked into inter-process stocks.

All these demand the maintenance of balance in System One. All are threatened by the disbalance induced by inter-elemental oscillation, which the Senior Management does not command the **Requisite Variety** to resolve by dictat on the central axis (although many such managements try this impossible trick). All actually use System Two devices —

inexpertly, because they are not recognized to be precisely ANTI-OSCILLATORY. So some are hopelessly informal, and some are too formal to react in time.

It is vital to understand System Two and its managerial embodiments. Here is the basic diagram:

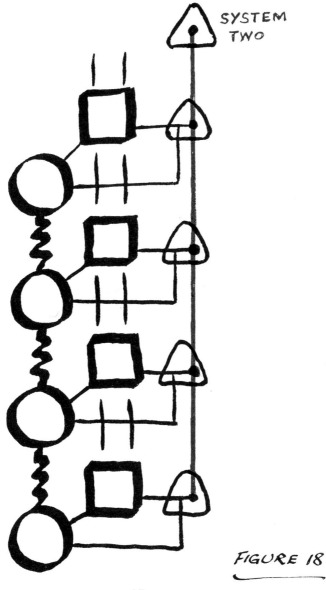

FIGURE 18

Note first of all that the top triangle is the **Regulatory Centre** for the **System-in-focus** — unlike the regulatory centres on the horizontal axes of System One, it is in touch with System One as a complete entity. The others are in touch with each other separately, as operational neighbours.

This is why the top triangle is drawn above the rest of the system in Figure 18: it belongs to the *next level of recursion*.

HOWEVER:

> System Two does not lie on the central command axis. Its function is not to command, but to damp oscillations.

> **NOW DO THIS:**
>
> Concentrate on your own System-in-focus.
>
> Think about the elements of System One, and concentrate in particular on the ways in which OSCILLATIONS might set up between them.
>
> There will surely be more than one mode of oscillation, and usually they will not be directly indicated by the 'organization chart' (which does not acknowledge the workings of Figure 17 in departmental correlates as a matter of necessity).
>
> List the modes of oscillation you expect on the left, and then list on the right organizational correlates or special activities that seem to exert a DAMPING effect.

Please do not cheat in this exercise by glancing ahead. There is no better way to fix the difficult concept of System Two as it is found — or may not entirely be found — in your own enterprise than by discovering about OSCILLATION from your own experience and insight.

There may be many surprises here.

The most accessible example of a System Two is

A SCHOOL TIMETABLE.

Think through its status and function carefully, and you may never make a mistake in analysing the role of System Two in any application of the VSM.

These are the main considerations:

- However you describe the System One of a school or a university, its departments or its faculties or its courses or its classes are each pursuing (correctly so) selfish ends which engage them in competition for scarce resources — notably staff but also other facilities.

- If each System One element were to determine its own programme unilaterally, then the whole plan for the future would be rife with 'double-booking'. The TIMETABLE takes care of this.

- ⊙ The timetable *reflects* managerial policies and decisions, but does not *make* them.

- It is accepted as authoritative throughout System One, because it does not seize authority, but is gratefully accepted *as a service.*

- The timetable is rigid in routine circumstances and is therefore a most convenient variety attenuator.
    > (Were it not for this, teachers would have no time to do anything except negotiate with each other.)

- The timetable is flexible whenever an element of System One is under duress
    > (if not, a teacher could not go for emergency dental treatment, say)

||| and its adaptations are *not then regarded as autocratic.*
THIS IS A REMARKABLE FACT.

ANSWER THIS:

What is the most obvious example of System Two in a Manufacturing Company?

Pause! and get it.

The answer to that question might have had to do with one of the accounting functions (see later), but the answer really expected was *production control..*

Read through the considerations on the last page, and note how closely the script will match this entirely different context:

We are in the presence of an invariant in the viable system

— its name is System Two
— its function is anti-oscillatory.

Bringing back from earlier pages the concept of invariance may have been startling: but there it is, and very powerful it is.

Bringing back the anti-oscillatory definition of function is more wearying than startling: but TAKE CARE.

There seems to be a compulsion on users of the VSM to cram all sorts of corporate activities into System Two — even when the job is not anti-oscillatory by any stretch of imagination.

This compulsion, doubtless, derives from the pressure to accommodate the institutionalized organization chart in this rendition. It is not a legitimate pressure.

ESPECIALLY:

- accountability does not reside in System Two
  — not routinely,
  — not through ad hoc enquiry;

- accountability, the discharge of the elemental role, is always to be found on the central axis — and is subject to its so-designed filtration.

NOW:
Look back three pages to the list of six major issues where oscillations threaten the equilibria mentioned. What are the System Two failures, vulnerabilities, and potentialities?

SPECIAL TERMS OF § FOUR

OSCILLATION   *failing to settle down in homeostatic equilibrium,*
a dynamic system over-corrects itself
continuously.

FOURTH PRINCIPLE OF ORGANIZATION

The operation of the first three principles must be cyclically
maintained through time without hiatus or lags.

§ FIVE

You are walking down the street, and someone is walking straight towards you. You will necessarily pass this stranger on his left or on his right. You make a tentative move towards your left; simultaneously *he* has veered to his right. A collision is in prospect, so *each* of you 'corrects'. You are now quite close to each other. Perhaps you will both 'correct' again. Some people often have the experience, and sometimes end up face to face with the other person — giggling nervously. (Others, a minority, say that they have never experienced any such thing: apologies to any such reader.)

Attention is directed to this example, because it is quite certain that no-one has a *policy* that determines whether to pass on the left or the right. 'The Management' has not 'taken a decision' about this — of course not: to do so would be a neurotic compulsion. Nonetheless, the result is that the pedestrian does not have requisite managerial variety to prevent the oscillation's setting in.

Anyone who took seriously the invitation of the last exercise should have begun to see how oscillations occur — either because there was no policy directive, or because the directives were made autonomously at the lower level of recursion and had no corporate consistency. But when people begin to perceive this in actual organizational settings, they try to supply the Requisite Variety that would offset the oscillations by corporate dictat on the central command axis. This is quite the wrong response. It uses up goodwill and the sense of freedom to no advantage. Witness: there would be absolutely no point in passing a law to compel pedestrians to pass each other on the left. They are not going to collide in any case — the nervous giggle mentioned is the highest penalty. (Because it is different with ships at sea, the equivalent rules *do* have to be made.)

Production control, we said, is a major example of an industrial System Two. It is concerned with a balancing act between the market demand on the one hand and manufacturing convenience on the other. Sales decisions and production decisions are *inputs* to the production control function; they are not the kinds of decision taken by the production controller himself. Those are about the best ways of doing things, *given* sales and production constraints. Sales and production directors inside System One knows that System Two has a better (i.e. overall) vantage point from which to help them meet **their own** desiderata. But it is not to anyone's advantage to do this at the expense of holding vast inter-process stocks, which tie up both capital and warehousing space. Most people with industrial experience will have seen how the oscillations set in (if the regulatory System Two does not work too well): material bays are stacked as high as the ceiling one day and are empty the next.

NOTE:

- The Production Controller does not have higher status than the System One managers: he has more knowledge about what is happening in the rest of the organization.

- While it is true that knowledge is power, in this case as in any other, the Production Controller's power is **limited** to anti-oscillatory regulation.

- The presentation of System Two should therefore not be threatening. It often is, because its true role is unclear.

Each System One is served by more than one System Two, because there are always several oscillatory sources.

NOW DO THIS:

Make a copy of the facing Figure 19 to represent your own System-in-focus. Annotate the square boxes you identified before.

Now find at least three Systems Two, entering these functions in the red boxes A, B and C.

74

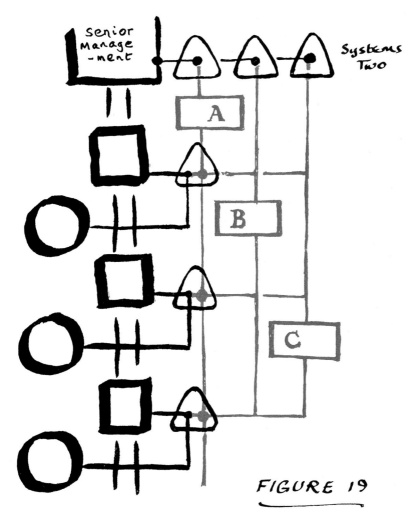

FIGURE 19

This is one possible convention for extending the diagram of the VSM model under development.

Observe that Systems Two must be dependent on the senior management, since they deal with the *whole* of System One.

They do not exercise authority in the ordinary executive sense, and there they are *not* shown on the central command axis.

FIRST EXAMPLE: Manufacturing Company

Senior Management —   Set above the divisional square boxes —
                         but often consists of or includes their
                         managers (cf. self-reference)

Square Boxes,   The divisions or departments
   System One —   themselves.

e.g. {
    System Two, A — production control (see text)

    System Two, B — the safety environment

    System Two, C — the personnel ethos
}

No misunderstanding here, please.

There are SAFETY RULES, which are promulgated down the
central command axis. These are direct variety attenuators. People
can be FIRED for not wearing hard hats in appropriate areas, or for
failing to use the guards on a machine tool. So System Two has to
do with a generally variety-attenuating environment, whereby
there is no oscillation between various parts of the works: we do
not expect different standards to prevail, nor one manager to take a
stance that would make another look either slack or overly
punctilious. This kind of safety environment is created by posters,
accident 'thermometers' that promulgate statistics, and so on.

> NOTE that both the command function and the anti-oscillatory
> function are probably handled by the same people. The
> distinction drawn here is none the less important. Indeed, the
> *command functions* of otherwise 'advisory' units may lose force
> if their System Two functions are disregarded . . .

There will be RULES about employment too; but the ethos as to the
firm's attitude to people also has a strong System Two component.
Think it through.

NOW: are the three examples (separately A, B, C) too formal or
too informal?

SECOND EXAMPLE: International Planetary Protection Agency

Senior Management —   International Board

Square Boxes,   National Boards
   System One —

eg. {
  System Two, A — international timetabling

  System Two, B — house style

  System Two, C — ethical consistency

By now it should be relatively easy to disentangle the command functions from the anti-oscillatory ones. An agency such as this will certainly disseminate policy decisions that partly determine A, B and C above. But the national boards will demand a lot of latitude in their interpretation, claiming autonomy in the light of local knowledge.

That is fine: but when will come the point where global *synergy* is lost for lack of shared arrangements that do not IN FACT rob System One of local initiatives?

Timetabling in schools has been discussed: similar arguments apply here — because of limited attention by the media, and therefore by the public. Names and emblems are valuable variety attenuators, for similar reasons. Thirdly, consistency of major facets in any organization across System One is an attenuator of major value; and although all enterprises have a general ethical 'colouration', in this sort of example a damping of oscillations in this domain demands particular care.

PAUSE   NOW TO DO THIS:

Consider your own System-in-focus.

Does it have something you would call

- a salary policy?
- a car policy?

Are these so-called 'policies' (which are expected to be **low** variety under this name, or its synonym 'guidelines')

- actually **high** variety RULES promulgated on the central command axis?

- System Two activities, preserving some local autonomy?

WOULD YOU LIKE TO CHANGE THE EMPHASIS?
- How?

- And how would you achieve this?

THIRD EXAMPLE: A Health Service

Senior Management —   The Health Authority (at whatever level of recursion)

Square Boxes,   general practice, hospitals, community
  System One —   medicine, and so on; or hospitals Alpha, Beta, Gamma; depending on the level of recursion.

Here (facing, Figure 20) is another diagrammatic convention

eg. System Two, A, B, C, D, E   • keep things flexible.
                                         • who knows how
Think about these five: many Systems Two you may uncover — *OR* conceptualize?

A and B are familiar by now. They are accepted and formal. Though whether they are well done or not is another question:

- Does A make use of **mathematical queuing theory?** (If not, maybe they still spell ante-natal with an 'i'.)

- Does B make **attenuating** use of computers? (If not, maybe you are generating another vast bureaucracy.)

C is interesting. Nursing protocol is not a matter of edict. It is essentially an anti-oscillatory device. And yet not even edicts have quite this FORCE. It is variety-attenuating to the point of systemic inanition . . . even death.

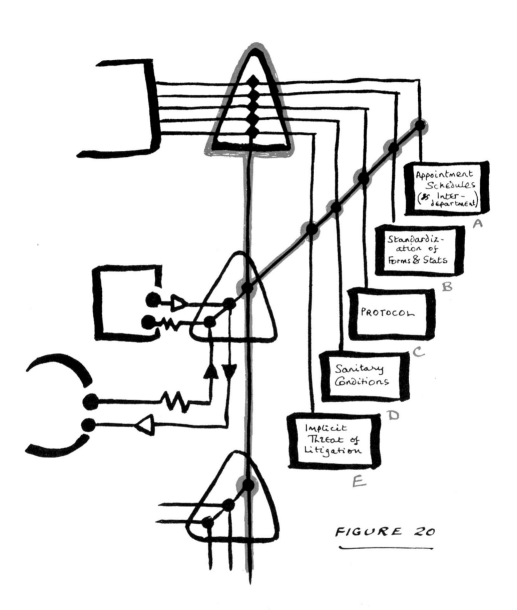

Appointment Schedules (& Inter-department)

A

Standardiz-ation of Forms & Stats

B

PROTOCOL

C

Sanitary Conditions

D

Implicit Threat of Litigation

E

FIGURE 20

79

How far is D a matter of edict, and how far a matter of accepted practice? If the latter is the predominant partner, then recognize that TRAINING POLICIES underwrite many Systems Two **from a higher level of recursion**.

> [This is most evident in the demarcation disputes that arise between Trade Unions in every industry. Think hard, and beyond political prejudice, to reach the machinery of this!]

E is a perfect example of the **unexpressed** System Two. A and B were formal, and recognized for anti-oscillatory devices. C is formal, but wrongly intuited (especially by patients, who see only autocracy). D is more complicated than it looks. So what is E?

> *NOTE*: to call E an anti-oscillatory device makes the issue of potential litigation open to discussion in cybernetic terms. Otherwise it is an emotive and political matter.

FOURTH EXAMPLE: A Family

Senior Management —   Pater Familias? Usually, some combination of Mother and Father.

Square Boxes,   Members of the family . . . but whom
  System One —   should this include (cf nuclear and extended families).

Looking back to Figure 19:

e.g.

System Two, A — mutual respect, indicated by: body language, explicit emotion, tricks and games . . .

System Two, B — shared understanding of 'what the neighbours will say'

System Two, C — shared awareness of what a dead grandfather (e.g.) would have said or done.

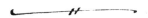

In the last Section (Four, page 64) an important process was begun. It was recognized that the elemental units of System One are proliferating variety on the horizontal axis of the diagram, and that there are **vertical constraints** on the freedom of variety generation. Four were listed:

    (i) the Corporate Intervention,
   (ii) the Resource Bargain,
  (iii) operational (squiggly-line) linkages,
  (iv) environmental intersects

— and by now these are familiar indeed. So too by now is:

    (v) System Two: anti-oscillation.

CORPORATE MANAGEMENT involves vertical constraint BECAUSE it too must have REQUISITE VARIETY.

As soon as the vertical linkages came under scrutiny, we saw that the Principles of Organization apply just as well to the corporate (vertical) management as to the elemental (horizontal) managements of System One. Then what have just been referred to as variety constraints are part of the **corporate management design**.

NOW DO THIS:

Bring the sketches of your own System-in-focus up to date, in a form that summarizes everything so far understood. In particular, ensure that the five vertical linkages are sufficiently well represented.

The question to answer now is:
    Does the Senior Management have REQUISITE VARIETY to absorb the variety proliferated by the horizontal elements of System One?

    — constrained as that is by the five vertical linkages.

In trying to answer this, NOTE that all five linkages refer to relationships that are **routine**.

It will be difficult to answer that question precisely unless a measuring system is developed (and that is by no means impossible). What you should find possible, however, is the assessment of the *relative* importance in absorbing horizontal variety that the enterprise gives to the various vertical channels. This gives an immediate 'feel' for whether the organization tends to be autocratic or democratic.

But return to the definite question about the Senior Management's deployment of Requisite Variety — and recall the hint just given as to **routine**.

All five vertical channels are filters of variety; and of course (i), (ii) and (v) have been specially designed to filter management information.

So the question must arise:
  what happens if what the management most needs to know is FILTERED OUT (by the use of totals, averages, and so on)?

Poor managements, having too little insight or training, or suffering from 'corporate paranoia' that has them feeling constantly threatened, disregard the filters, and try to restore Requisite Variety on the central axis. That is, they disregard the resource bargain (where in principle the homeostatic message upward needs to be only 'OK'), and invigilate the horizontal activities with all the zeal of an Inquisition.

But there is a whole set of acceptable management practices that do not involve this centralization of manifest power, which — properly designed — are capable of generating enormous variety. Such mechanisms work **sporadically** (not as a perpetual routine — see previous hint), and — by agreement with System One management — penetrate straight to the operations themselves.

These procedures, which may generically be called 'audits', are indicated as the sixth vertical channel in the facing Figure 21 — marked in red.

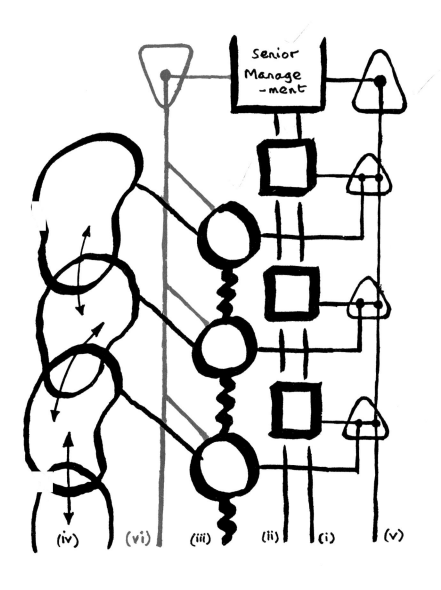

Senior Manage -ment

(iv)　(vi)　(iii)　(ii)　(i)　(v)

FIGURE 21

83

Now it is open to us to deduce from the Law of Requisite Variety that vertical homeostasis must obey:

The First Axiom of Management

The sum of horizontal variety disposed by all the operational elements
EQUALS
The sum of vertical variety disposed on the six vertical components of corporate cohesion.

Most people worry about the manipulation of varieties that they cannot precisely measure. Too much of the accountancy culture has entered into our regulatory thinking:

- how do you know that there are 'the right' number of bricks in a wall, to ensure that its top does not display gaps? Did anyone count them?

- you have just overtaken another car. How could you have applied 'the right' pressure to the accelerator without knowing the pounds per square inch to exert?

It is the same with matching complexity through the concept of variety.

CONSIDER:

Vertical channels (Figure 21) (iii) and (iv) absorb whatever variety the circumstances of the enterprise dictate. Channels (i), (ii) and (v) absorb whatever variety we have *designed* them to absorb — given our management style ((i) and (ii)) and the proneness to oscillation (for (v), or System Two)

Then because of the Law of Requisite Variety, as expressed above in the First Axiom, it NECESSARILY FOLLOWS that

Variety of Audit Channel (vi)
= Total horizontal variety generated by System One *minus*
Varieties (i) + (ii) + (iii) + (iv) + (v).

The Audit Channel CLOSES THE GAP.

84

As the name 'audit' implies, some of this work will be done *routinely* in its sense as *regularly*. But audits do not have to be routine in any other sense of the word; and this is exactly what makes this channel both necessary and sufficient to 'top up' the requisite variety of senior management in any given state of play.

In fact, and would-be auditors in the above wide-ranging sense should note this, routine and regular audits surrender a large part of the variety they generate to no purpose whatsoever. Think of the way in which WW2 Prisoners-of-war escaped from Germany, by doing their digging in the gaps between rigorous patrolling . . .

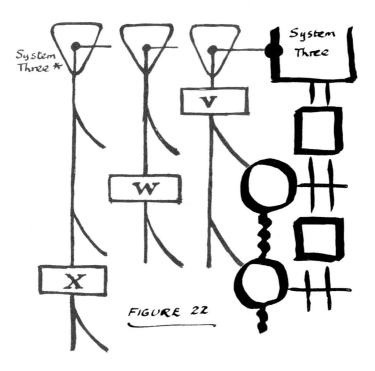

FIGURE 22

There are no surprises here . . .

NOW DO THIS TOO:

for your own System-in-focus

That aspect of Senior Management which deals with all the matters so far discussed emerges from Figure 22 with the name of System Three. It is different from System One, because it surveys the System as a totality — which the component horizontal elements are not placed to do. It is different from System Two, because it exerts authority on the central command channel.

System Three, then, is responsible for the *internal* and *immediate* functions of the enterprise: its 'here-and-now', day-to-day management.

Then it is responsible for, although it does not conduct, the anti-oscillatory functions of System Two.

It is also responsible for the activities we have just been considering, which it may well conduct, in the sense that these are sporadic, high-variety, intra-operational, 'task force' activities **defined in terms of** the System Three need to replenish its own Requisite Variety. This is why they are called System Three* (Three-Star) — they are not separable from Three itself, except for the fact that they operate — by consensus — APART from the command function.

e.g. {
System Three *, **V** __ 'management audit': how are we placed for succession
System Three *, **W** __ a special survey of the state of all our buildings
System Three *, **X** __ a Work Study enquiry into the utilization of electric motors, their makes and spares.
}

You may have realized, in undertaking these exercises, that the ACCOUNTING function offers the most obvious examples of all aspects of management considered in these cybernetic ways. Then good news and bad news:

- **Good**: this confirms the overriding importance of accountancy in managerial regulation — which is a fact, and must be reflected;
- **Bad**: The accounting profession, not having studied managerial cybernetics, makes no distinction between the four roles shown next — and gets a reputation for autocracy in return.

It would be useful now to draw the following diagram on a large
sheet, and to fill it in with your main findings. Of course, my
showing five examples on each of the managerially-designed
channels is quite arbitrary.

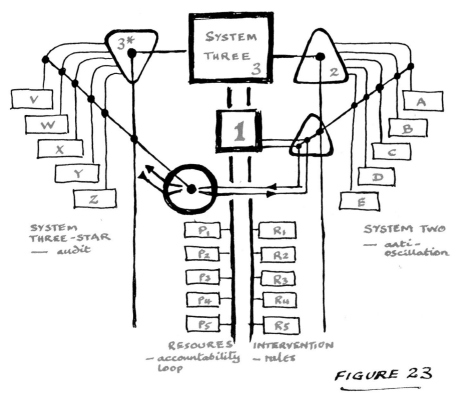

FIGURE 23

P's are essentially PROGRAMMES.
R's are essentially RULES.

COMPLETE a copy of Figure 23 for your System-in-focus

• ENSURE that ACCOUNTING functions are
thoughtfully represented.

SOME NOTES ON ACCOUNTANCY

When accountants turn their minds to these ways of looking at their profession (and quite a few have been known to do so) they often declare changes in the *presentation* of their activities.

The FINANCIAL DIRECTOR does not give much of his time to System Three, unless he is also the Chief Accountant — who fits this role ('here-and-now') precisely — and especially in an enterprise that has climbed out of the straight-jacket of 'historical casting' in favour of 'management accounting'. So we get (Figure 23):

RULES: SYSTEM THREE $\rightarrow$ ONE: R_1, R_2, R_3, etc:
These are the interventions that enable the Senior Management to discharge its legal responsibilities: they determine the form and meaning (in particular) of the Balance Sheet and the Profit and Loss Statement.

RESOURCE BARGAINS: SYSTEM THREE $\leftrightharpoons$ ONE: P_1, P_2, P_3, etc:
These are the arrangements made to distribute resources and obtain ACCOUNTABILITY for them. Program Planning and Budgetting (PPBS) Systems typify these bargains.

ANTI-OSCILLATION: SYSTEM TWO: A, B, C, D, E, etc:
These are essentially the costing techniques that supply standard costs, variances, and so on. The accountancy principles and practices involved are OPEN TO DISCUSSION. This can easily be CONSENSUS rather than DICTAT management.

AUDIT: SYSTEM THREE-STAR: V, W, X, Y, X, etc:
These ad-hoc, high-variety activities are well understood, and are to this extent already consensual.

NOTE THIS: The Internal Auditor (on channel 3*) is highly knowledgeable about System One: he may be so **identified** with it as to forfeit independence . . .

HOWEVER: The External Auditor comes from a *higher level of recursion* (whether on an institutional or simply a professional basis). He gains in independence what he may forfeit in detailed knowledge . . .

— what a combination!

A REVISION OF SPECIAL TERMS

Please note that we have come all this way on the strength of only a dozen special terms.

Then resist the opposition of those who say: 'this stuff is incomprehensible'. It means simply that those people are unwilling to stop and think, or to question their own prejudices.

Let us review this small vocabulary, and confirm that we fully understand it:

§ ONE
p. 17

Viable
Recursion
Self-reference
Homeostasis
Invariant

§ TWO
p. 35

Variety
Requisite Variety
Attenuator
Amplifier

§ THREE
p. 53

Channel Capacity
Transducer

§FOUR
p. 71

Oscillation

§ FIVE
p. 89

and here we are:
NONE

The First Axiom of Management

The sum of horizontal variety disposed by all the operational elements
    EQUALS
the sum of vertical variety disposed on the six vertical components of corporate cohesion.

§ SIX

The notion of hierarchy cannot be altogether escaped in discussing the viable system, although all our enquiries constantly reveal the equivalent importance of the five major subsystems. It really is not survival-worthy to have a brain that would support an Aristotle or a Newton or a you, if any of the major organs or physiological systems (such as the endocrine) closes down. Similarly, a Senior Management group whose factory falls down or whose country is blown up is rendered dysfunctional too.

The reason that we still cannot escape the notion of hierarchy is the existence in all viable systems, which are after all always *enterprises*, of an equation of power. The will for survival seems to be what governs this equation. And whether we look at animals, in which the brain 'commands' the nervous system and (in man at least) 'masterminds' the will to survive, or at social institutions in which some Truman is always effectively saying 'the buck stops here', acknowledged hierarchies emerge.

Hence it is that most people say of brain-damaged people that they are like vegetables, and surely they would be better off dead. Few are found to wonder, although some do, whether these folk are not 'nearer to God'. Equivalently, most folk say that societies must arm themselves in order to resist enemies, because it would be better to die than to lose their freedom, although there is no agreement about the word 'better', and no agreed definition of freedom either.

All right: This is not a dissertation on philosophy, and most readers are likely to be happy enough with the concept of hierarchical management. The fact is that I am not, and that the above paragraphs are spattered with inverted commas and stylistic reservations with good reason and serious intent. Cabinet ministers and even Presidents of nations have deplored to me their impotence-in-practice; and not for nothing is a poem echoed in many a Boardroom that begins: 'I wish I knew whether I were Chairman of this Company'. But, yes, only the most senior of senior managers arrive at these insights, if they ever do;

while those who have no compunction in abusing as well as exercising power are certainly able to demonstrate the force of hierarchy to unarguable effect. Then my final remark shall be only to note the lack of wisdom in using pathological states of systems as means of *defining* (rather than to *diagnose*) healthy ones.

We saw that it is System One, and not 'Senior Management', which **produces** the viable system — which generates its wealth. We saw that a System Two would be needed to damp the oscillatory behaviour inherent in the structure of System One. And now we have arrived at the requirement for System Three, which has the *role* of observing the One-Two complex from the privileged position of (*intra*systemic) omniscience. This role is a necessary condition of viability, and our enquiry has to treat it as such . . .

> NOTE THEN: System Three is not constructed as a box to house people with better suits and bigger cars than anyone else. That they do have these things is simply the result of a general acquiescence in the hierarchical concept.

> A BIT MORE PHILOSOPHY: Go and look into a monastery if you doubt this. System Three still works without the perks. But in real (?!) life it suits the greedy to acquiesce in greed: their turn (they hope) will come.

With all of this introduction we may ask, *not* that you should find the company organization chart to see who is running the show and their relative seniorities, but that you should

MAKE A LIST

of the System Three components of your System-in-focus.

That means:
- Who are those who partake in Resource Bargaining, the allocation of resources, the Accountability Loop;

- What supportive management does each have to administer the A, B, C, D, E . . . activities of System Two;

- What supportive management does each have to initiate and conduct the V, W, X, Y, Z . . . activities of System Three Star ?

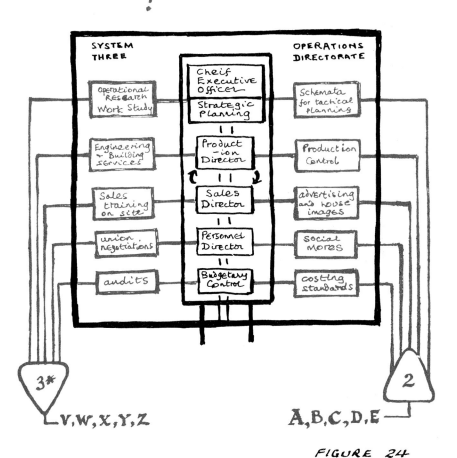

FIGURE 24

Figure 24 is an illustration of an answer.

It is disappointing for two reasons:

- It is a generalized statement (it has to be) — yours should be much more specific, idiosyncratic, YOU-ish.

- It is not, inside itself, very **systemic**. Look at the feeble attempt to emphasize a needed homeostat between Production and Sales! What are all the real connexions in your own example?

Please: you should not by now have the least inhibition about drawing an elaborate system inside your System Three box — a diagram full of boxes and arrows, all homeostatically arranged, and all obeying the (four) Principles of Organization. I cannot do this for you any longer because I don't know what your System-in-focus *is*. Earlier on, it was possible to guess about (what are after all) fairly standard inter-relationships on the horizontal axis. The *items* in Figure 24 are fairly standard, too; but the relationships now reflect the power equation of the vertical axis.

> NOTE: There is nothing inconsistent here. If we were to shift a level of recursion down, we should find a System Three in each element of System One . . .
>> . . . but we didn't treat it like that: our recursive vantage point was different.

Finally, in relation to your work on Figure 24 (the last exercise): make sure that there is no confusion between the A, B, C, D, E *activities of System Two* and the within-Three senior management bases that underwrite them, nor between the *System Three-Star* *activities* V, W, X, Y, Z and the within-Three senior management bases that commission those. There is a risk of confusion here, because a similar nomenclature is inevitably in use, but —

> **REMEMBER** the difference between
>> System Three — commanding, making decisions — on the central axis, and
>>
>> System Three — enhancing its capacity to absorb variety, via Systems Two and Three*.

To bring the lesson home, look back over page 88 about the four modes of accountancy regulation, and

> **ANSWER THIS:**
>
> How would you **demonstrate** the minimization of 'dictat', and the emphasis on 'service', in financial administration — as revealed by the variety analysis of Section Five?

A possible answer is that you might use different colours of paper for the documentation of the four systems. In particular, if the Intervention channel's colour were red, then System One would discover how **little** red paper there is — and how justifiably important. Senior financial managers often have little idea of the animosity their 'manuals' often engender . . .

. . . and other senior managers, although they may not issue 'manuals', may well by their behaviour antagonize System One without having the slightest idea of the reason.

Take a look at this picture of *your own* System One, generating horizontal variety:

We already know from the First Axiom of Management that all of this variety, V_{horiz}, must be capable of absorption by System Three — using the six vertical channels we have discussed.

How this is done, and how it will be seen to be done, are different matters: the concern is with managerial STYLE.

NOW DO THIS:

Refer to Figure 21 (page 83) on which the (finally) six vertical variety absorbers are shown.

Determine for your System-in-Focus how the First Axiom (horizontal variety = vertical variety) appears to be met

- as System Three sees it;
- as System One sees it.

Be honest. Talk informally with those concerned. There are ALWAYS surprises in this exercise.

Is it possible that the answers look anything like this? If so, we have an example of what a psychologist would call COGNITIVE DISSONANCE.

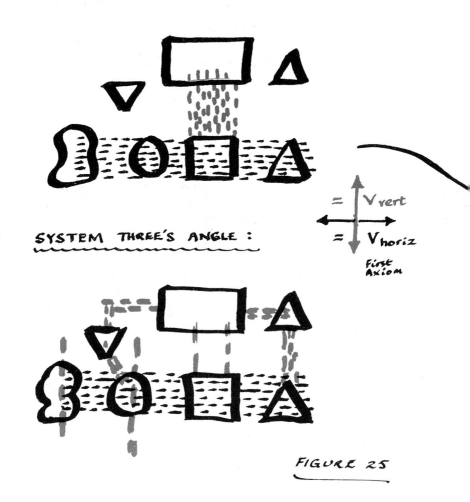

SYSTEM ONE'S ANGLE :

SYSTEM THREE'S ANGLE :

FIGURE 25

The First Axiom is obeyed in both cases;

> the 'objective' facts are the same . . .
> but System Three feels saintly,
> System One feels oppressed.

Feelings of oppression are very real when System One's variety, so much needed to provide requisite variety on the horizontal axis

> (however is the management box to absorb the higher variety of the operations, or to direct those so as to absorb the even higher variety of the environment? — remember?)

is, or even feels as if it is, wholly absorbed by System Three.

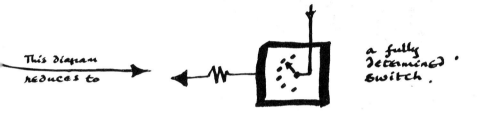

In such case, it would be better to replace the System One management by a computer — because it is not free to face variety with its own creative variety, but has to pretend that 'the world' is really the outcome of a simple formula.

> *And* this is just what is happening — from the management of the economy, to the lack of choice in consumer goods — in contemporary Western society.

NOW CONTEMPLATE THIS:

Is it the case that all conceivable horizontal variety generated by System One needs to be taken into account in **any** of the variety equations?

How have you in fact been deciding what is to count in them?

The question is disingenuous: step warily.

Variety is the number of possible states of the system. Today, Fred Bloggs has changed his shirt . . . Well, it is clear that from the start (when we first began to consider equations of variety) we must have adopted some **criteria of relevance**. Yes: but how has the process of relevance-noting been maturing in recent exercises?

It is a familiar managerial question to ask whether all relevant *variables* that affect *outcomes* have been detected in the *operations*. Was the last question posed reduced to that? If so, it does not lead to the most fruitful answer.

What matters in discriminating one 'state of the system' from other states is whether the resulting **change of state** serves, or has no bearing on, the **purposes** of the system.

> NOTE THE DIFFERENCE between this formulation and the previous one. It is much more fundamental.

Now we have not spoken of the system's purposes before, except in declaring its viability — and therefore the implied purpose TO SURVIVE: this is the 'separate existence' of the 'recognizable entity'. But usually the viable system has a purpose imposed upon it, thus:

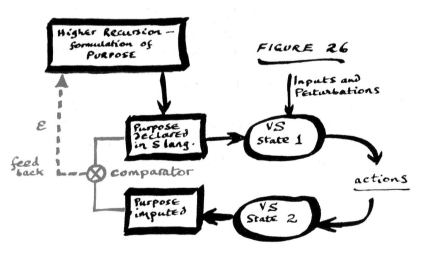

FIGURE 26

Look first at the black part of Figure 26.

It is usual for the viable system to have a purpose formulated for it within a higher recursion, and this purpose must be expressed in the *Language* that the system (S) understands. Note that in dropping a recursion, because then of the need for transduction, the *statement* of the purpose may change.

Inspired by this purpose, and required to act by its proper inputs and the perturbations that assail it, the viable system's State 1 produces actions — and for itself a new, resultant, State 2.

A GOOD OBSERVER will **impute** the purpose of the system from its actions and thus from the resultant state.

Hence the key aphorism:

⊓ The purpose of a system is what it does. ⊔

There is, after all, no point in claiming that the purpose of a system is to do what it consistently fails to do.

Again, then, we are likely to encounter COGNITIVE DISSONANCE. To suggest how this is in practice resolved, electrical conventions are again used — in the red part of the diagram.

A comparator, naturally enough, continuously compares the declared purpose with the purpose imputed from the results that the system delivers. This results in the *feedback* of an error signal ($\mathcal{E}$), which will modify the original statement of purpose.

> NOTE: 'Feedback' is improperly used to refer merely to *response*, which is how most managers use the term. Feedback generates **corrective action** (whether positive or negative).

> THIS SYSTEM WILL CONVERGE ON A COMPROMISE PURPOSE — it is neither what the higher recursion would most like to see done, nor what the viable system itself would most like to indulge in doing.

NOW IDENTIFY

The compromises of purpose in which your System-in-focus is implicated.

Can you really settle for these ❓

Obviously this complication about purposes has implications for the process of *planning*.

For the time being, these remarks refer to the planning of System One by arrangement with System Three — which we know as Resource Bargaining, and ticketed in Figure 24 with the label 'strategic planning'. (We are not yet talking about corporate planning for the whole System-in-focus.)

All planning is a continuous process leading to the commitment of resources now, that the future may be different.

For what purpose?

It is here that our convergence diagram (Figure 26) comes in useful, for many of the planning protocols around ignore purposes altogether, and assume *agreed objectives*. However, the agreement about objectives is a spin-off from the convergence on purpose.

The purposes of the corporate system and those of System One are different, because System One consists of viable systems whose conditions of survival are formulated at a different level of recursion. In principle, the higher recursion can cut off, or sell off, a System One; and this in turn (because it is capable of independent existence) can in principal leave.

So long as the System-in-focus is to remain cohesive, the compromise convergence must continually act. Its trajectory takes it towards
the lowest variety compromise possible.
This is not a surprise — since no sort of negotiation piles on unnecessary complexity — but it is an outcome whose importance is often overlooked.

NOW DO THIS:
Take the compromise on purpose identified in the last exercise, and evaluate how far its bias is toward the purposes of the whole System-in-focus, and how far towards the purposes of System One.

The scale could be:
100/0   80/20   60/40   50/50 . . . and so on.

The measure selected (subjective, rough, though it be) tells you about

the authoritarian character of the enterprise.

All viable systems conform to the laws of viable systems; but they are markedly different in the number of states of the system (i.e. its variety) that they regulate.

This is the underlying reason for the apparent differences between and among animate and inanimate systems (e.g.: brains and computers), individual and societal systems (e.g.: people and groups), goal-seeking enterprises and service-oriented institutions (e.g.: firms and government departments).

There is NO NEED therefore to have different classifications, and different organizational theories, for all these systems — SO LONG AS they are all viable systems.

This argument is sensational! It denies all the hallowed academic categories with which professors assault each other ...

The differentiation can be done in terms of:

- the amount of variety under regulation at all;

- the distribution of regulatory variety between the central command axis (two) and the other four vertical channels.

AND ALL OF THIS will be determined by the **convergence of purpose** for the System-in-focus.

PLEASE:

Go back to the question at the foot of page 94, and reconsider it —

and also the subsequent questions to this point.

This question asks you to take part in a **convergence of purpose** exercise . . .

So? Who gave them the authority to repeal the natural laws of viable systems?

All that was intended as an experiment in 'iterative programmed learning'. The idea was to get up enough speed to jump a very considerable hurdle: a false notion of purpose left in our path by about 2000 years of categorization and reductionist thinking — and reinforced recently by naive (though expensive) management consulting.

So where have we arrived; and could you now accept these statements — based not only on argument, but on your personal experience of answering the questions?

■ WHEN WE KNOW

what is: **the purpose of the system**
which is: **what the system does**

(after convergence between

$$\frac{\text{System Three}}{\text{and System One}} = \text{strategic planning})$$

■ THEN WE MAY ALSO KNOW

the criteria for distinguishing possible states

— meaning:
how to measure variety.

■ THIS WILL THEN TELL US

how much variety the First Axiom must necessarily handle,

■ AND IT WILL DETERMINE

the **minimum variety** on the vertical command axis ●━━━━
transmitting regulation that guarantees COHESION in the viable system.

means the **freedom remaining** to the management on the horizontal axis to manage.

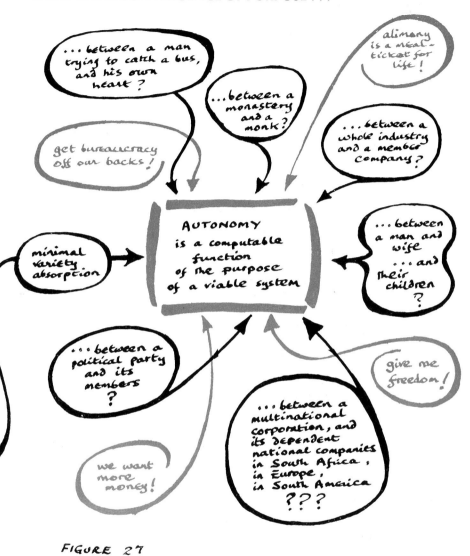

FIGURE 27

HOW TO INTERPRET THE SLOGANS
IN TERMS OF SUCH AUTONOMY?

The previous page is not offered by way of decoration.

There are statements about the nature of autonomy, which is a topic of crucial importance in organizational structure, on pages 102 and 103 that relate autonomy to systemic purpose. Figure 27 displays six (black) questions about the convergence of purpose between two levels of recursion, and four (red) questions that require exactly that same background of understanding before the slogans that they incorporate can be properly addressed.

NOW DO THIS:

Consider the black questions in turn, but also in relation to each other:
how do you assess the degree of autonomy of the embedded system in each case?

Consider the red questions relationally too:
search out a real feeling for the sense in which apparently absolute exhortations involve recursive logic and ordinal measurement of variety.

There are manifest personal and political inferences that can be drawn from examining emotive topics in a scientific way. One needs to be rather brave: the idea of 'computable functions' encroaching on accepted notions of personal freedom or artistic vision or spiritual growth is anathema to most people. Yet all three are subject to limitations that can be measured.

To look closely at the structure of organizations, the entailments of one thing by another, the complexity of problems in relation to available analytic power . . . Such approaches do not change the nature of the freedom or art or love that they examine. But they may offer a degree of sanity in handling practical affairs, and even a mode of spiritual realization, that is not automatically accessible to someone who simply declares himself liberal, liberated or loving. How aggressive such humility can be!

Let us take our own autonomy seriously, at each level of recursion where we recognize ourselves **to be** — and recall that no-one can compel us to choose between arts and science, liberty and law, one love and another: homeostasis is something else.

SPECIAL TERMS OF § SIX

COMPARATOR   *a device that compares one numerical value with another, and marked thus:*

FEEDBACK   *the return of part of a system's output so as to modify its input.*

(Feedback is not *'a response to a stimulus', as in popular usage.)*

NOTE: *In particular then, as we saw, an error signal whereby a* comparator *sends* feedback *to the initiating recursion will eventually result in the*

CONVERGENCE   *of the states compared, such as* ^{A}and ^{B}above.

AUTONOMY   *the freedom of an embedded subsystem to act on its own initiative, but only within the framework of action determined by the purpose of the total system.*

105

§ SEVEN

All the emphasis recently has been on the idea that the organizational structure so far examined, which maybe we can simply call 'the 3-2-1', deals with the *inside-and-now* of the organism — the System-in-focus.

Shift your grip on the business of recursions, hold on tight, and formulate an exact answer to this

QUESTION:

Since the 3-2-1 of the System-in-focus deals with the *inside-and-now*.

Why did we spend so much time looking at **environmental** relationships?
(Remember, e.g. Figures 5, 6, 7)

The answer is that the environmental relationships concerned were NOT THOSE of the System-in-focus as such. They were the connexions of System One. As *such*, these belong to the next lower recursion.

It is particularly important to keep this point in mind in considering all matters of planning and adaptation. The fact is that the sum of all the System One environments is **less than** the total environment of the System-in-focus. Not only is it 'less than' in the sense of 'not including so much'; the environment of System One is (by definition) the environment of the existing operational enterprise, whereas the environment of the whole System-in-focus belongs in another level of recursion.

A careful study of the next diagram (Figure 28) ought to bring this home. Remember:

- The *black* part of the picture is the 3-2-1, the inside-and-now of the viable system;

- the *whole* diagram stands for the System-in-focus;

- We are used to talking about 'the Senior Management'. What the diagram tells us is that SYSTEM THREE **constitutes part** of that.

- The rest of Senior Management has to cope with the big red environment . . .

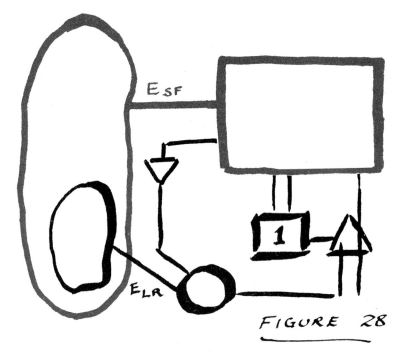

FIGURE 28

Well, all this certainly presses the original point of this Section:

the environment of the System-in-focus is not the sum of System One environments.

As so often happens, our own bodies provide good examples of viable systems (as well they might!).

The various organs of the body have micro-environments that need to be kept in homeostatic view by the **autonomic** (good name) nervous system. The truly automatic system of adaptation will stop me from falling over, keep my water balance in good order, increase my respiration as necessary, and so on. It will also promote volitional action at an almost subliminal level. 'Come to think of it' (I can say, reviewing the last hour or so) 'I must have switched on my desk light, and put another log on the fire, since I started this Section . . . I didn't really notice . . .'

In this way the organization keeps its day-to-day enterprise going. But it is abundantly clear that I am more than the sum of these activities — and that is because my environment is more than the set of micro-environments that work on my external organs (like the skin), and work *up* from my internal organs, notifying the state of equilibrium in the 'interior milieu'.

I am going to Philadelphia on Thursday week, and on to Vienna after that. My skin does not know this, nor do my intestines. Something in my viscera *does* however know: it is reacting to a premonition of high endeavour, and we call it 'excitement', or 'anticipation'.

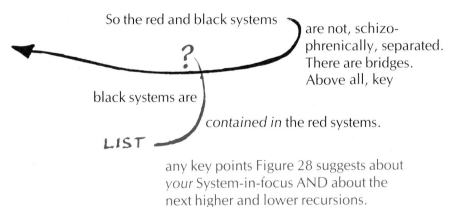

So the red and black systems are not, schizo-phrenically, separated. There are bridges. Above all, key black systems are *contained in* the red systems.

LIST any key points Figure 28 suggests about *your* System-in-focus AND about the next higher and lower recursions.

All that can be offered by someone not involved about answers to that question is that

- ● the next-lower recursion is in System One (refer to Figure 4), and its environment is the 'black' environment of Figure 28.
- ● It has plans within that compass.
- ● Then what does it NOT perceive about the 'red' environment in which it shares?
- ● What moves might the Senior Management be considering that are BEYOND THE IMAGINATION of System One?

- ● the next-higher recursion has the RED Box of Figure 28 as its System One; and it has an environmental envelope about two metres high.

:} see above, in the opposite direction.

NOTE: Never reckon that 'lower' recursions are less important, less able, or (especially) more *stupid* than 'higher' ones. Differences are **appropriate**: the roles, the histories, the responsibilities, the technologies, and (in summary) the LANGUAGES of different recursive levels are different. So to say (above) 'beyond the imagination' sounds pejorative, but is not so intended. It seems clear from their utterances, for example, that royalty and prime ministers find the lives of ordinary people 'beyond the imagination'. That they do not know this, nor believe it, is a confirmatory point. At any rate, the same points hold in *both* directions of the hierarchical embedments of viable systems.

SERENDIPTY — ADDENDUM

Imagine a play in which a minor character has only two words to say (though many times) — *yes*, and *no*.

Now imagine another play, in which its director is rehearsing the actor concerned in the first play. In this second play, the actor again has only *yes* or *no* to say — many times.

Contemplate the fun generated by GRAHAM GREENE, whose twenty minute play I heard at this precise point in the book, when all the yeses and noes belong to two different but entangled levels of recursion . . .

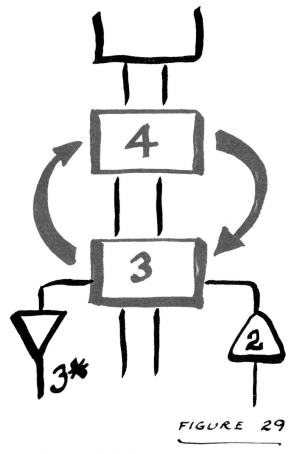

FIGURE 29

Life is full of cybernetic clichés . . .

The one we now address is the above homeostat, and the argument is simple enough.

If System Three has been discriminated within Senior Management as responsible for *inside-and-now*, then we shall also need to discriminate a System Four — to deal with (let's call it) the *outside-and-then*.

111

NOW DO THIS:

Take a sheet of paper on which to list all the activities of System Four — the *outside-and-then* of your System-in-focus.

Make headings like this:

Unit
Activity   Responsible   THEN =   Concern

Under 'Then =' put 'C' for current, or a number for the number of years ahead that fruition seems likely.

Under 'Concern' put A, B, C, D or E — where 'A' recognizes the highest priority. (This is not an ordering: everything could be classified as 'A', or 'E'.)

A special test in comprehension and/or seriousness of intent is bound into this exercise. Therefore it is more than usually important to do the work **before** glancing forward in the text.

Actually write out the list, or you will not be able to submit yourself properly to the test.

Number the items listed. How many have you detected? Is *that* all?! Is that enough activity to guarantee adaptation to the future?

REVISE THE LIST

in the light of these extra remarks.

If you have by now satisfied yourself that you have done a good and thorough job,

TURN THE PAGE

and read the box headed 'Here's the Test', on page 114.

BACK AGAIN?

It will be surprising if you have not made a mistake — and correcting a mistake is a powerful way of learning. Hence all the palaver about concealing the clues on page 114.

Well, in an extreme case there could be nothing left of your list. Or maybe you have been encouraged to evolve a new one. In any case (for we have surely grasped by now that systemic diagrams are more likely to generate ideas than mere lists), here is the next task.

GROUP

the listed activities into *major areas* that are themselves inter-related by their *common implication* in the response system of the enterprise;

DRAW A DIAGRAM

showing how these *thrusts into the future* overlap.

This (Figure 30) is the kind of diagram that really works, and that also repays much re-drawing. Because the TOTAL INTERSECT (coloured red) defines the centre of the enterprise's real concern about its future (these may be more than one such centre); and because *each* intersect points to the need for collaboration (hatched on the diagram to illustrate two examples).

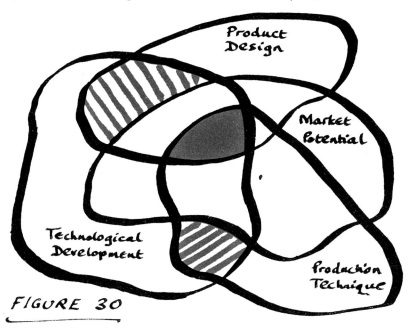

FIGURE 30

113

Not in the interests of creativity alone is the drawing of this diagram (or set of such diagrams) advised. The managerial cybernetics is important too.

Consider a few major activities that probably figured in your lists/diagrams:

- Research and Development (namely, Technical R & D),

- Market Research,

- Corporate Planning . . .

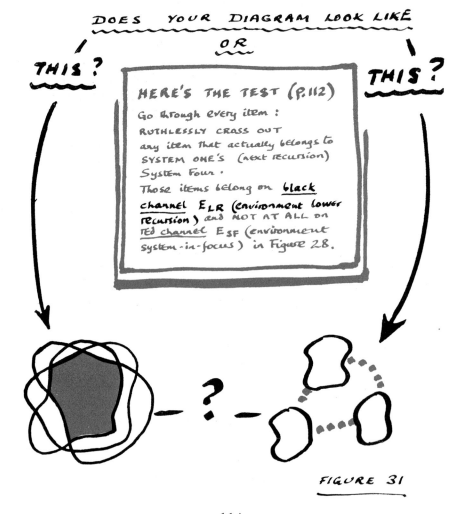

DOES YOUR DIAGRAM LOOK LIKE
OR
THIS?   THIS?

HERE'S THE TEST (P.112)

Go through every item :
RUTHLESSLY CRASS OUT
any item that actually belongs to
SYSTEM ONE'S (next recursion)
System Four.
Those items belong on **black**
channel E_{LR} (environment lower
recursion) and NOT AT ALL on
red channel E_{SF} (environment
system-in-focus) in Figure 28.

FIGURE 31

The second, quite disconnected, diagram is the most common —
and, if that is close to yours, then something should be done about
it most urgently. In fact: how can it be? The answer has to do with
professional pride, or even obsession:

- R & D is in a well-established and academically
  prestigious area of scientific competence. It tends to
  follow its technological nose, regardless of

- Market Research findings, which are much more
  entrepreneurially oriented, and are based on the self-
  image of attenuator/amplifier on the environmental
  loops.

- Corporate Planning has become part of applied
  economics. It will consider the relative merits of
  alternative policies in terms of 'pure' discounted-cash-
  flow budgets — as if the R & D and market research were
  simply inputs to a computer programme.

In short, even the dotted red lines (down below, on the facing
page) may be an exaggeration of the reality — a total disjunction.

What we have to do is to constitute our Figure 30 as a

model of its own (that is, System Four) self.

This conclusion is pointed to, with underlinings, because it is
another example of that difficult notion we called *self reference*.
Nor is it an example alone: it is the operational basis for the final
self-referencing, system-closing, System Five to which everything
is now leading.

SYSTEM FOUR is not only concerned to *manage* the *outside-and-
then*, but to provide self-awareness for the System-in-focus.

SKETCH A DIAGRAM

— before turning the page — of a notional System Four that
reflects these matters.

How do you visualize it?
What are the key features?

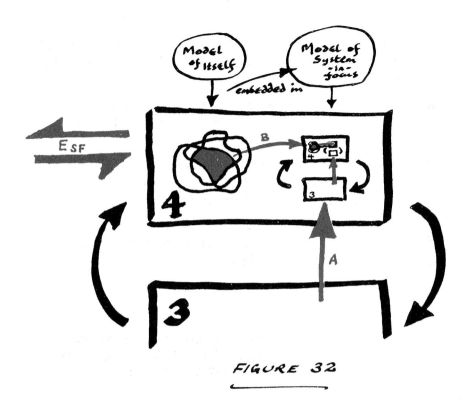

FIGURE 32

No doubt you captured the idea of the model of its own activity's being embodied in a model of the whole System-in-focus. Did you also realize

- The account of the *inside-and-now* is filtered upward via System Three — arrow A.

- The System Four model of itself arrives in a model of the whole of System Four — arrow B.

- So System Four of the System-in-focus contains a model of that System Four, which contains a **recursive model** (see small copies of A and B) — indefinitely . . . **?**

As hinted earlier, it is just this infinite regression of self-images that seems to hold the key to the characteristic **self-awareness** of viable systems.

116

The question as to how System Four should best be embodied and made manifest within the Senior Management is not one for this particular book.

- At best, we need some kind of **management centre** (I have also called it an **operations room**), and the machinery of that is discussed in *Brain* and *Heart*.

- At least, we shall need to establish linkages that will do the best we can about Figure 31 as we have actually found it to be, working towards the left hand figure.

> [But, oh please, do not simply constitute those red dotted lines as a bunch of committees. **They will not have Requisite Variety.**]

- *ANYWAY*:

> The Three-Four Homeostat that obtrudes so forcefully on our consciousness in Figure 29 MUST OBEY THE FOUR PRINCIPLES OF ORGANIZATION.

> It cannot be said too often.

> Nor can it be over-emphasized that they operate on all **vertical** homeostats (such as Resource Bargaining), as well as on the horizontal ones where they first became familiar.

So in this case, we have to check on *channel capacity* (Principle No. 2), and requisite variety in the *transducers* (No. 3), and the *dynamics* of everything (No. 4) — all of which propose problems implicit in the red-dotted sentences above.

VERY FEW ENTERPRISES have a well-functioning System Four. EVEN FEWER conform to the Principles that govern homeostasis.

QUESTION:
What happened to Organization Principle NUMBER ONE?
   Consider now its impact.

● The First Principle of Organization talks about the EQUATION OF VARIETY as it diffuses through an institutional system.

● Now recall the Axiom of Management in which we argued that the sum of horizontal variety in System One is absorbed by the sum of (the six channels of) vertical variety. This is a measure of variety in System Three.

● Then where the Three-Four Homeostat is concerned, it follows from the two notes above that:

The Second Axiom of Management

> *The variety disposed by System Three resulting from the operation of the First Axiom*
> > *equals*
> *the variety disposed by System Four.*

CRUDELY THEN:

Investment of (yes) **money**, (but also of) **time, care, talent, attention, reward** must be properly balanced, homeostatically.

Too much of this investment in Four, and the *inside-and-now* of the enterprise may collapse beneath your feet.

Too much of this investment in Three, and you may be making the world's best buggy-whips, in which (notoriously) there is no future. The *outside-and-then* will go ahead without you.

PICK OUT A FEW DISASTERS:

Even though you 'know the cause', try running the facts through the Three–Four Homeostat rules . . .
Usually this procedure will 'give an explanation' that throws *managerial* light on otherwise *technical* factors.

e.g. The Rolls Royce collapse: the RB 211 engine was churned in the Three–Four vortex, whatever the financial complications as such.

Of course we are left with this problem: how to apply the Four
Principles of Organization to the 'supra-environmental' loop. We
first met this on page 27 (Figure 7), promising to discuss it later.
Well, here it is, in a minimal enlargement of the loop E_{SF} of Figure
28.

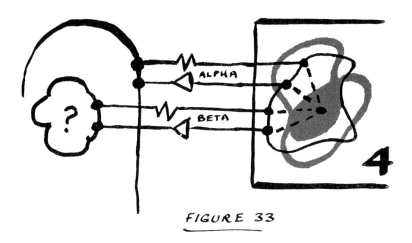

FIGURE 33

In Figure 33:

The black outline in Four is just *one* of the set of outlines
considered earlier. EACH OF THEM needs its own Alpha and
Beta loops — not shown except for Black.

The Alpha loop projects (amplifier) its image on the environment
of the *outside-and-then* as a continuous concern. What is going
on that is relevant to us? — then we must mark that with our
presence and our commanding knowledge and plans. The input
arm of the loop (attenuator) needs designing as a 'forward
observation point': no use waiting for fortuitous information.
Not only must this loop be closed by the black outline (the area
of this particular interest), it must also be closed — see dotted
lines — within the intersect of all System Four interests.

All of this applies also to the Beta loop; but this is anchored in
THE UNKNOWN FUTURE. Hence the '?'.

119

The Alpha and Beta loops really do face quite different problems. Monitoring what is actually happening in the big wide world, and correctly assessing the *trends*, is different from being alert to NOVELTY. Folk too often assume that the future will be an extrapolation of the past — and then someone invents the transistor. Folk too often assume that they will see the relevance of the NOVEL without special preparation: the evidence is that they will laugh it to scorn — and then get taken over, attacked and beaten, or simply rendered bankrupt or extinct.

So the details really must be designed. Start with Figure 30, and develop both Alpha and Beta loops for the *outside-and-then*. But bear in mind Figure 32. Figures and Principles and Axioms all come together, to distribute variety in equal amounts both vertically and horizontally. Only now then can the issues be addressed holistically — that is, without generating suboptimizations either vertically or horizontally.

NOW DO THIS:

Make the clearest possible statement about the DESIGN of variety handling on the red lines shown

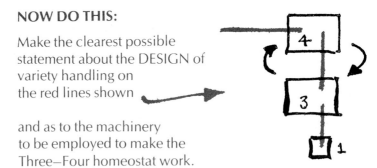

and as to the machinery to be employed to make the Three–Four homeostat work.

Recollect

- The various variety balances must be held steady.

- The *rate* at which they operate to restore equilibrium must match the mean rate of perturbation.

- Every attenuation of variety risks the loss of vital information, or the introduction of ambiguity.

- The Three–Four homeostat is the organ of ADAPTATION for the enterprise.

SPECIAL TO § SEVEN

Once again, there are no special terms to list and remember.

Take back some alternative 'homework' from this section, then, by reviewing the following allegation:

> *When an enterprise comes under threat, among its early responses is the cutting back of System Four . . .*
>> *'. . . we don't have either the time or the resources to worry about all that now . . .'*

this being (supposedly) the organ of adaptation.

On the face of it, this reaction is suicidal; if it is not, then System Four was either unprofessional or its Senior Management was not in good faith.

The Second Axiom of Management

The variety disposed by System Three resulting from the operation of the First Axiom

> *equals*

the variety disposed by System Four.

§ EIGHT

The last action called for was a difficult one. Not much help is possible, because the design of all those filters is content-dependent — and I just do not know what your business is.

It is certain, however, that the variety reductions involved are enormous; and that *whatever* we do by way of attenuation will run us into major risks, stemming from the resulting skimpiness of variety — and the paucity of information defining that variety.

One of the systems in which this problem has been formally studied for a long time is the game of chess. The number of possible plays is great, which is what makes it interesting; but the rules proscribe much of the variety proliferation that would otherwise occur: the queen cannot swerve in the course of one of her straight-line sallies, for example, and the knight cannot make more than one of those peculiar little jumps in one go. You might think that the analysis of chess, which received a tremendous boost from computer-power, is too formal or stilted an enterprise to have bearing on management: not so. It is because of the mathematical **invariances** of which we have spoken before.

Bear with me then; and even if you are not a proper chess-player

ANSWER THIS:

Suppose that a chess-game has been well opened-up, and that neither side is at all obviously in the ascendent. There is a huge number of possible moves and strategies open to you.

How do you think that you would **attenuate the variety** of the situation?

The expected pause for thought will surely have revealed that you need to *eliminate* considerations about certain pieces, certain areas of the board, certain possible tactics of the enemy, and to *concentrate* on others. That will reduce variety, and is a necessity . . . but **how**?

Years ago, having formulated a theory supposing that good chess players can recognize patterns, and thereby instantly discard huge tracts of variety, I had a series of discussions with one of the grandfathers (and in my case godfathers) of cybernetics — he was a world authority on the brain. My hypothesis was bolstered by the experimental fact that players who had made a lifetime's study of standard plays, and historical games, and the opinions of masters, were more successful in ordinary chess than those who had not; whereas in versions of chess such as 'kriegspiel' (in which these advantages are largely lost, because the player is kept in ignorance of the opponent's moves) the expert's pattern recognition was no better than the less expert's.

Warren McCulloch's reply, however, declared that there was *no way* of recognizing the pattern, whether expertly or inexpertly, without considering and grading every possible move. The brain could do this easily, he contended, though not consciously — in the time available. What we choose to call 'pattern-recognition' is an acquired skill that can be developed only because (at some level of consciousness) we 'know everything'.

Now we left System Four trying to design a filtration system that would recognize pattern in the unknown (but developing, immanent) future. *Can* it review everything, however cursorily? Somehow or other, surely, it has to acquire criteria of relevance. In McCulloch's chess case, after all, we **know the rules**.

I think that the rules come from System Five: not so much by stating them firmly, as by creating a corporate ethos — an atmosphere. Some firms have indeed published formulated 'objectives', but (from experience) this is not recommended. It is virtually impossible to steer a course between these two shipwrecking rocks:

- motherhood statements:
  'we shall act within the
  law', 'guided by the
  shareholders'
  interests' . . .

- 'We shall do THIS, and
  none other' —
  regardless of what may
  happen in an unknown
  future?

Therefore let us approach the *closure* of our viable enterprise in System Five like this:

'ethos' —
a variety
sponge

FIGURE 34

Even in these days (providing management with an ambience of less authoritarian attitudes promoted by behavioural science) 'the boss' still exists. As we said, using President Truman's phrase: 'the buck stops here'. Besides, and despite our essentially decentralizing cybernetics, the heads of enterprise *do* preserve certain rights of decision — although some of them feel that these rights are limited to decorating their own offices in bizarre ways.

But the point about the *ethos* concept is that it is a **variety sponge** of gigantic capacity. Try to think of a really way-out idea in your organization — so way-out that certainly no-one has ever considered it, although it is not manifestly daft.

HOW WOULD THE BOARD REACT TO THAT?

The betting is that you know the answer exactly. No-one has put the idea forward just *because* the answer is self-evident. This is not to say that the answer is correct.

125

It is not difficult to see that this variety sponge in System Five helps to attenuate the variety of System *Three* — because System Five knows very well what the **existing** business is. But no-one knows what the future business will be: if they think they do, they are riding for a fall (just look at international politics).

HOWEVER: those people know something about it; and it is this very something that constrains the apparently unconstrained System Four. The pattern-recognition emerges McCulloch-like from an ethos that has, *in some sense*, 'seen it all'.

NOW DO THIS:

List the contents of System Five in your own System-in-focus.

I·N·T·E·R·R·U·P·T *If you got no surprises here, do it again . . .*

The Board is one element:
    how exactly does the board behave?
    What are its levels of power?
    Who is on it who should not be on it?
    Whom would you add to it?

How about the *Chairman* of the Board?

We are really finding out about ETHOS now.

Pause to return to chess.

Since Warren McCulloch's death (and although in his lifetime Samuels and Shannon and many others devoted great efforts towards computerizing chess) the Soviet Grandmaster and former World Champion M.M. Botvinnik published his conclusions. It is completely impracticable to review all possible permutations of a game: it would take 30-followed-by-twenty-nine-noughts years, reviewing a million positions a second. And managing an enterprise is far more complicated than chess. However, the number of legal moves open to each player at each turn averages about 30. So analysis to a 'depth' into the future of two half-moves involves 900 possibilities. Going to four half-moves means studying a million variations, with perhaps a hundred computer operations for each. Since this four half-move approach is about the limit of computer effectiveness in reasonable time, and since important variations in chess often involve more 'depth' than this, then (argues Botvinnik) other means of variety attenuation than straightforward 'decision-making' must be involved.

The 'strengths and weaknesses' analysis by which managers are often invited to *seize opportunities* is therefore not strictly possible. The manager will have to take chances, and this (despite much propaganda) he is most unwilling to do. Chess players are much the same.

Botvinnik's conclusion is this: until the 'depth' picture resolves itself at a level where one can legitimately take a decision, the proper course is **to strengthen oneself**.

Managers seem to intuit this to some extent. Unfortunately, strengthening 'oneself' is however often seen as the need for strengthening the inside-and-now, the 3-2-1. But System Four is also part of 'oneself'. Moreover, System Four is the very part that will develop the 'depth' picture that has to be resolved. Botvinnik is perfectly clear that the decision not to act **is a current action**.

In terms of the VSM, what we are discussing is the INTERVENTION BY SYSTEM FIVE in the balancing activity of the THREE-FOUR HOMEOSTAT.

NOW DO THIS:

Recapture the 'way-out' idea you considered only two pages ago.
We 'knew' how the Board would react to that (although the Board has not said a word).
Trace now *exactly how* the Three–Four homeostat is being affected by the TOP LEVEL ETHOS

- by taking the profit-earning Three more seriously than the money-spending Four?
- by determining what kind of Four filters with the environment are legitimate?
- or what?

It must now be apparent that we are by now dealing with 'ultimate authority': System Five. Then why did this Section not blow all its trumpets, and announce the primacy of the Board (or whatever) — as by implication does the Organization Chart, with System Five sitting on top of the dunghill and crowing? Why start with off-hand talk about chess, and smuggle in a boss-figure in a fog of 'ethos'?

The fact is that in a viable system all five subsystems are dependent on each other. And if any has a special primacy, it is System One — because it consists itself of viable systems. This is not organization-chart talk at all. But it is real-life talk.

REMEMBER?
'The purpose of a system is what it does'.
And what the viable system *does* is *done* by System One.

System Five, then, is 'only' thinking about it.

But if System Five in me were *not* thinking about it, I should not be going to Philadelphia shortly (as earlier announced): I should be staying here. And if System Four had not first entertained a model of possible actions, which included going to Malaysia instead, then System Five might have had nothing to think about — and no decision to take. System Five would, by its *somnolence*, have endorsed System Three's decision to keep the 3-2-1 going on its current occupations. 'Somnolence'? But surely this would have been the **decision** not to act that is the current action . . .

The oblique approach to System Five is meant to encourage caution and hesitancy in a matter in which we are conditioned to obsequious endorsement of the mere claims and trappings of power. Yet the power is real enough. So the question is: who really wields it?

Before saying more about that question, it would be well to consider how far the argument has come in terms of Figure 35 — facing. This conceeds the inclusion of a boss figure in System Five, who may still *decide* things, and issue *orders* on the **vertical** red loop shown. But, as was argued earlier, this is not the main function of 'the ultimate authority' —

which is:

- to supply logical closure to the viable system; and

- to monitor (see the **outside** red loop) the Three–Four Homeostat

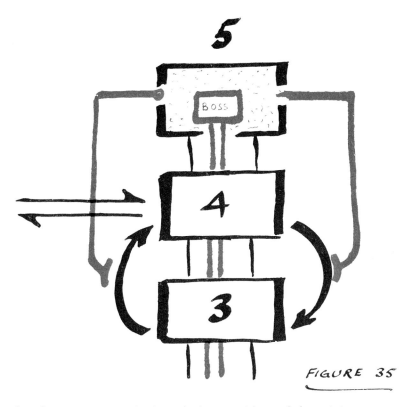

FIGURE 35

The above structure deals with the *outside-and-then*. It is **metasystemic** to the 3-2-1. We may call it the 3-4-5.

These are convenient appellations:

and they emphasize a vital fulcrum at System Three (which, for this reason, usually thinks it is running the whole enterprise).

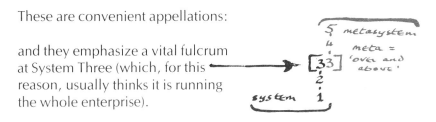

We have said 'closure' several times in the text. Logical closure means above all

> - self-reference: the assertion of **identity**.

It also means

> - there is **no more**.

If anything has been missed, it is — by definition — missing within this framework.
There could not be a 'System Six' — because the five-fold system is a *closed* system, in logic.
(It is obviously *open* to both energy and information.)

One way of looking at this is to see that the 'variety sponge' at Five is *mopping up* variety that the homeostasis of One–Three and Three–Four will not have accounted for. The tidy equations of variety presuppose models of everything that *expresses* that variety (even if they cannot precisely calculate it). But beyond our best accounts of what happens, is Botvinnikian 'depth'.

So — as the First Axiom of Management asserts the horizontal and vertical variety equivalence of System One, and as the Second Axiom asserts variety equivalence inside the Three–Four homeostat —

The Third Axiom of Management says:

> *The variety disposed by System Five*
> *   equals*
> *the residual variety generated by the operation of the*
> *Second Axiom.*

We often think of what is 'left over', residual, as being very small. There is nothing to stop it from being very large indeed.

System Five may be absorbing more variety than anyone has realized. How about doing the work suggested on pages 126 and 127 all over again? *YES : DO IT !*

PAUSE for a moment.

It is not for chess this time, but for the third oldest University in the United Kingdom: St. Andrew's — it comes third only to Oxford and Cambridge.

St. Andrew's has a 'boss', called the Principle, and powerful he is. But the equivalent of the Board in a British University is the Court. At St. Andrew's the court is presided over, not by the Principle, but by the Rector. And the Rector is elected by the **students**.

It is a popular supposition that this set-up is a joke — because the students elect (for example) comedians: professional comedians, not idiots. But whom else should the students elect? They have enough Establishment characters in the offing already. Two famous comedians have recently been Rectors of the University, and it seems that they did not regard the appointment as a joke at all. They regarded themselves as actually having influenced affairs. Well: *both* of them graduated in law from Cambridge . . .

The Chairman of the Board (like the other Directors) **claims** to represent the shareholders. They elected him or her.

The country's President, or Prime Minister in Britain, **claims** to represent the people. They elected him or her.

NOW DO THIS:
Consider for

 • your own System-in-focus

 • some other sample systems — such as government
the extent to which

 SYSTEM FIVE is or claims to be none other than
 SYSTEM ONE.

 [Ha! Of course: the Chairmen of all our
 subsidiaries are Corporate Directors!]

THINK ABOUT the relevance
 of the Law of Requisite Variety.

THINK ABOUT the operation
 of the Four Principles — particularly No. 4, about lags.

 [Ho! I was **elected**, and my term is to last
 for 4, 5, 7 years . . . when do I need to
 start worrying about the next election?]

It will be sad if, after reading this whole text to this point, and having probed the nature of System Five for nine pages, the point is not now quite made:

SYSTEM FIVE 'masterminds' a metasystem called 3-4-5, the *outside-and-then* management.

To discover what this truly involves —
- SHIFT the window on the set of recursions of the viable system that you have been calling the System-in-focus UP ONE LEVEL.

- The metasystem 3-4-5 is now SYSTEM ONE of the new System-in-focus.
  And what *is* a System One?

- Turn to page 1 of this text, and start work.

Figure 37, on page 135, puts the whole VSM together, and fully illustrates the above finding — which is in my opinion very exciting, and potentially productive. It leads straight to:

The Law of Cohesion

(for multiple recursions of the viable system)

The System One variety accessible to System Three of Recursion x

    equals

the variety disposed by the sum of the metasystems of Recursion y for every recursive pair.

ANSWER THIS:
Have you seen this LAW OF COHESION before, in any form?

Let's hope you got it right. It is none other than the First Axiom of Management, expressed in the language of the System-in-focus.

What else would you expect of a recursive system?

There is a last feature of the VSM to incorporate: it is extremely important, but there is not much to be said — so don't flick the page too soon.

We were speaking of *somnolence*. It is an occupational hazard of System Five. After all, all those filters on the main axis . . . maybe Five will hear the whole organism droning on, and simply 'fall asleep'.

For this reason, a special signal (I call it **algedonic**, for pain and pleasure) is always identifiable in viable systems. It *divides* the ascending signal — which we know to be entering the metasystemic filtration arrangements — coming from System One, and uses its own algedonic filter to decide whether or not TO ALERT SYSTEM FIVE. The cry is 'wake up — danger!'

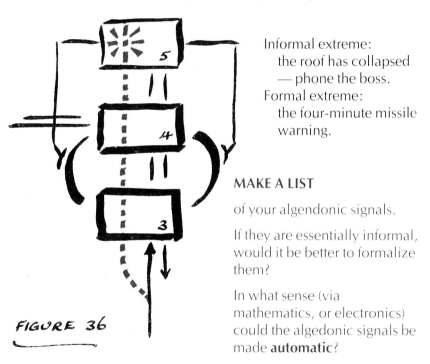

Informal extreme:
    the roof has collapsed
    — phone the boss.
Formal extreme:
    the four-minute missile
    warning.

MAKE A LIST

of your algendonic signals.

If they are essentially informal, would it be better to formalize them?

In what sense (via mathematics, or electronics) could the algedonic signals be made **automatic**?

FIGURE 36

133

SPECIAL TERMS OF § EIGHT

METASYSTEM a system 'over and beyond' a system of lower
logical order. (Higher authority is not the issue,
and may not apply.)

ALGEDONIC (ἄλγος, pain, ἦδος, pleasure); pertaining to
regulation in a non-analytical mode; raising alarm.

The Third Axiom of Management

*The variety disposed by System Five
equals
the residual variety generated by the operation of the
Second Axiom.*

The Law of Cohesion

*for multiple recursions of the viable system
The System One variety accessible to System Three of
Recursion x
equals
the variety disposed by the sum of the metasystems of
Recursion y for every recursive pair.*

Reference:

Botvinnik, M.M. — Computers, Chess and Long-range
Planning,
Longman, London, 1971

COMPLETION

OF THE VIABLE SYSTEM MODEL

The diagram on the next page ought not to look too daunting now. It has a special virtue. Not only are the recursions exact replicas of each other (such diagrams have been published before), but the way in which the five subsystems connect with each other *across* the recursions is also shown. The cross-recursion linkages of 3-4-5 are part of the ordinary reporting system — but remember that they have different **spheres of interest** (especially System Four). System Two and Three-Star require cross-recursion coordination of a delicate kind — if autonomy is to be preserved. Hence

FINALLY, DO THIS:

Make a detailed analysis, with lists, of the linkages across the *three* recursions shown in Figure 37, for *each* subsystem of the viable system. If they do not severally exhibit Requisite Variety, what shall you (in each such case) propose?

NOW TURN THE PAGE

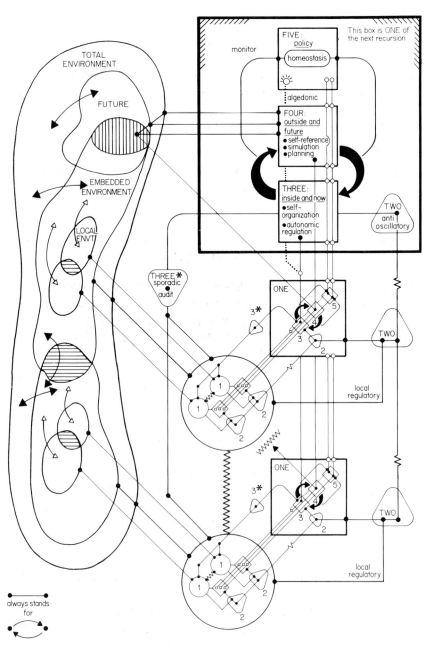

FIGURE 37

THE VIABLE SYSTEM
— Stafford Beer

APPENDIX

Readers who have made a first pass through the book making their own drawings have learned the hard way how tiresome it becomes to repeat the rather elaborate designs that reflect the structure of the Viable System. They have the advantage that the structure will have stuck in their minds.

Most readers, however, have probably noticed this Appendix in advance — and will proceed to rob themselves of a learning experience . . .

CERTIFICATE

The author of this book, Stafford Beer, and its publisher, John Wiley & Sons Ltd, hereby authorize the reproduction of all the Charts contained in this Appendix. This permission does NOT APPLY to the text itself, nor to the Figures 1 to 37 included in it.

All readers are in fact encouraged to photocopy the following Charts, and to make themselves a Do-It-Yourself Kit:

- make up pads, or tablets, of each chart, so that rough analyses can be made, torn up, and improved upon without fuss.
    Note: you will need more copies of some charts than others. Give this some thought before proceeding.

- if you have access to enlargement facilities, by all means USE THEM.
    Note: on a VSM chart 'blown up' to several feet high, it is often possible to give a succinct account of an organization, and its diagnosis, that would take a report several hundred pages long to 'explain'.

137

CHART ONE

This chart should be **named** for your System-in-focus — that is the total chart.

Then **annotate** the chart to show clearly what are the *included* viable systems (although only two of them are depicted). Make a few notes on these embedments, too, so that it is clear, for instance, what the tiny operational circles are supposed to be.

Next, **annotate** the chart in the area of the big square box, which is the management unit of the next higher recursion in which your viable System-in-focus is *embedded..*

> Note: Although the topology of this diagram is quite correct, the visual presentation really calls for this box to be standing on one corner. There was no room for this: don't be misled.

It is more difficult than people imagine to keep the System-in-Focus *in focus*! Therefore a fair copy of an enlarged Chart One should go up on the project room wall, preferably in colour, to keep all concerned alert to the set of recursions that has been chosen.

> A SPECIAL PLEA:
> You will obviously be using Figure 37 as a guide to annotating your own Chart One, as well as earlier Figures. But please don't just copy down the generalized words I have been forced to use. Try to make your annotations specific to the organization you are modelling.

> AND REMEMBER:
> These boxes are not boxes on an organizational chart, into which you might expect to fit individuals or departments. In particular, senior managers all have dealings in Three, Four *and* Five.

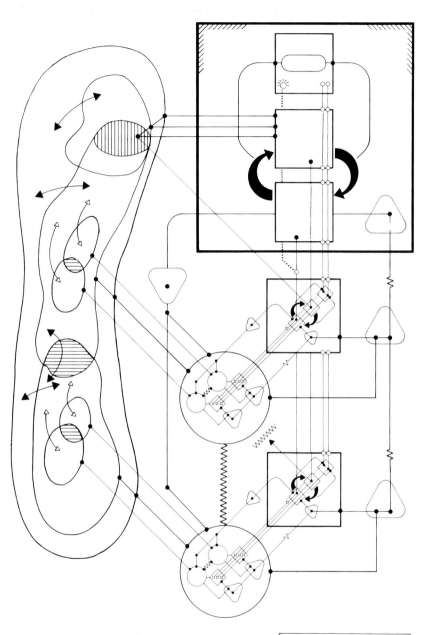

CHART ONE

CHART TWO

This chart, spread over two pages, is the main account that you
will construct of the viable systems included in your organization
at each level of recursion.

For the sake of illustration, think of a corporation, having
divisions, having companies.

RECURSION ONE

Write 'Corporation' in the box opposite, because this is the
System-in-focus.
Call it Recursion No: 'ONE'.
Its Name remains 'Corporation'.

How many Divisions are There?
Let us say **six**.

Three divisions are depicted on the facing page, and two
more on the page that follows. We are one division short,
when we stick the pages together.

By photocopying the facing page twice, and using scissors
and paste, four rather than three divisions can be created to
add to the two divisions on the following page. And so on:
maybe you need ten.

NOW START WORK

on the five subsystems
and your variety analysis

see Chart Three.

AT ALL TIMES keep the System-in-focus in mind. This is
Recursion One, the Corporation.
Those embedded systems are **divisions**, not companies.
Companies do not figure at this level of recursion. What is
more:

EVEN THE DIVISIONS

are black boxes.

So any detail you write in the ○ □ spaces will relate to
CORPORATE management of those divisions, and not to
DIVISIONAL management itself.

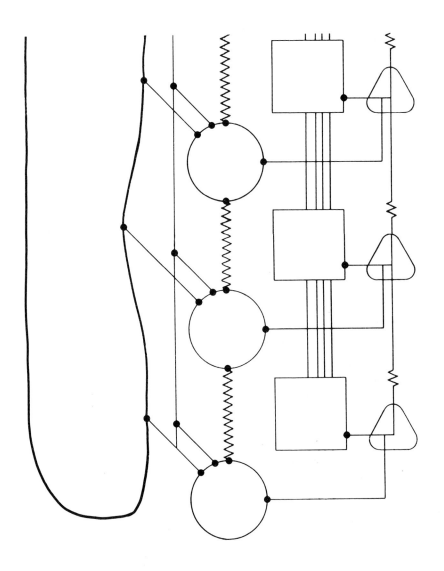

CHART TWO

Divisional management itself is of course to be handled at

RECURSION TWO

There are six divisions (we said), so we need six charts.
Take the first of these charts.
Write in the box under System-in-focus, 'Division'.
Write Recursion No: 'TWO/A'
Write the NAME of the first division.

The embedded Systems One are now the member Companies
of the Division. We must construct the scissors-and-paste
Chart Two from this facing page and the next to reflect the
appropriate number of Companies in the Division.
The rest of the instructions already given apply again.
You will end up with Charts for Divisions TWO/A through to
TWO/F — if you are undertaking an exhaustive modelling.

CONSIDER HOWEVER

that it may (for whatever purpose) be necessary to model only
a DIFFICULT Division-in-focus, or a TYPICAL Division.

RECURSION THREE

The System-in-focus is now the Company, that belongs to the
Division, that belongs to the Corporation.
Just suppose that each Division has six member companies.
Then there will be thirty-six charts for Recursion Three . . .

. . . unless it is unnecessary to study (say) more than one in
each division.

It is all a question of Requisite Variety. It is the reality-out-
there, and not the cybernetic technique, that generates the
work.

RECURSION NOUGHT

This is the name conveniently used for the Industry (say) in
which the Corporation is embedded. It needs to be studied, as
argued in the text; but not to call the Corporation itself
Recursion One may be confusing.

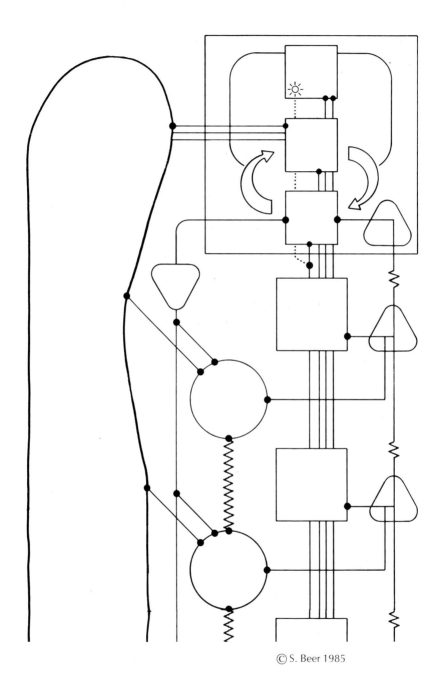

© S. Beer 1985

CHART THREE

There is no 'correct' interpretation of the VSM. We have spoken instead of more or less **useful** interpretations.

Even so, there may well be *in*correct interpretations, in the sense that the model's power to account for viability may become **denatured** by their use.

In practice, this is nowhere more likely to occur than in Systems Two and Three Star.

Chart Three is provided to help with the analysis. It is close to Figure 23 on page 87, and the arguments in the text should suffice. Use as many boxes as needed.

REMEMBER

- System Two is concerned only with the regulation of oscillatory behaviour;

- The Three Star channel represents
    — sporadic
    — high-variety
intervention in actual operations.
Audit is a typical 3* function.

RECALL

The FIRST AXIOM OF MANAGEMENT (p. 84).

On Chart Three we have two of the six vertical channels available to management to absorb horizontal variety.

They really do need to be designed, in relation to the two command channels that are central to regulation in Charts One and Two.

NOTE: The two remaining channels on the vertical axis are the 'squiggly-line' operational loops, and the environmental connexions. Both of these require special design treatment, depending on the situation studied. That is why the environmental box in Chart Two has been left blank. It requires elucidation and proper linking (on the model of Figure 37).

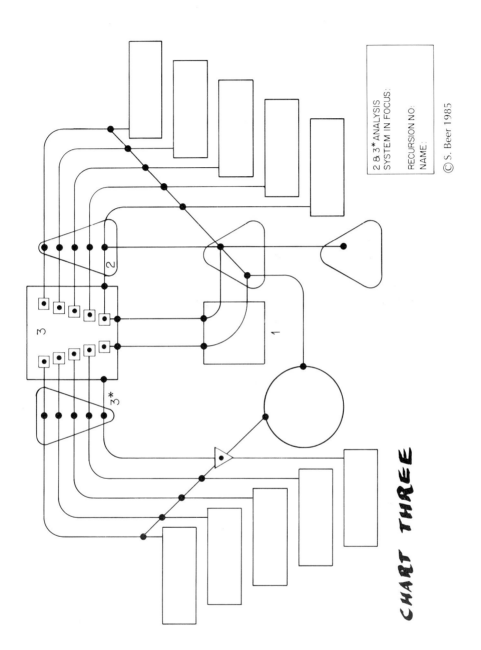

2 & 3* ANALYSIS
SYSTEM IN FOCUS:

RECURSION NO:
NAME:

© S. Beer 1985

CHART THREE

145

CHART FOUR

On the fundamental Figure 37 appeared this reminder:

always stands
for

— which is to depict a homeostatic loop.

THE FOUR PRINCIPLES OF ORGANIZATION
were enunciated so that homeostasis could be quantitatively
evaluated.

They dealt with VARIETY
- between blocs
- along channels
- across transducers

and with the whole process as exhibiting
- appropriate cyclical dynamics.

On Charts Two and Three, any straight line joining two points
marked with a large dot stands for a homeostatic loop. Hence

— in any VSM with its multiple recursions, there are
literally *thousands* of homeostats that we expect to
work, each being susceptible to cybernetic analysis.

This is a sobering thought: but management is not the child's play
its critics suppose.

WHEN IN DOUBT about the effectiveness of a homeostatic loop,
analyse it with the aid of the facing Chart, and check that the
FOUR PRINCIPLES apply — and are actually effective.

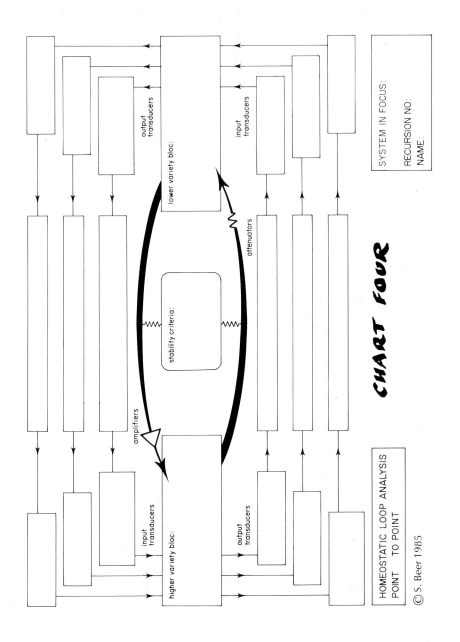

CHART FOUR

output transducers

lower variety bloc:

input transducers

attenuators

stability criteria:

amplifiers

input transducers

higher variety bloc:

output transducers

SYSTEM IN FOCUS:

RECURSION NO:

NAME:

HOMEOSTATIC LOOP ANALYSIS
POINT TO POINT

© S. Beer 1985

147

AN EXAMPLE OF CHART FOUR IN USE

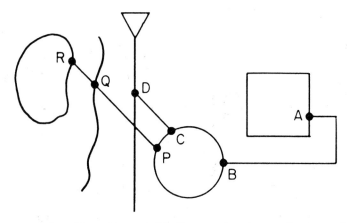

Suppose that Chart Two yields in part the above. Seven points are nominated; they, with the lines between, depict four homeostats.

A ●————● B is the management-to-process loop

C ●————● D is the System Three loop 3*, marking audit-style interventions in processes

P ●————● Q is the homeostatic loop connecting the process to the general environment

P ●————● R more specifically connects to (let us say) the *market* subset of the general environment.

Then the Chart Four tabulation on the facing page is an analysis of the homeostat connecting points P and R.

Follow each loop round, and note

- attenuators and amplifiers are 'two sides of the same coin';

- requisite variety (R.V.) is the quantifiable unit involved at all times.

- the three (arbitrarily three) rings will in practice impinge on *each other* — therefore

- 'causality' is a concept of little use in systems theory or cybernetics.

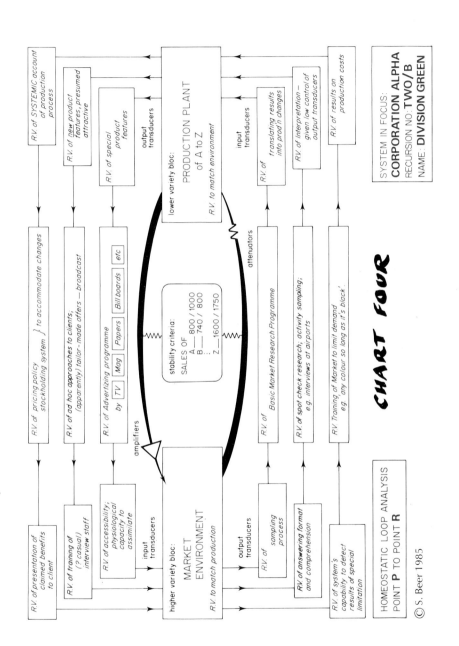

CHART FOUR

SYSTEM IN FOCUS:
CORPORATION ALPHA
RECURSION NO: **TWO/B**
NAME: **DIVISION GREEN**

HOMEOSTATIC LOOP ANALYSIS
POINT **P** TO POINT **R**

© S. Beer 1985

R.V. of SYSTEMIC account of production process

R.V. of new product features, presumed attractive

R.V. of special product features

output transducers

lower variety bloc:
PRODUCTION PLANT
of A to Z
R.V. to match environment

input transducers

R.V. of translating results into prod'n changes

R.V. of interpretation — given low control of output transducers

R.V. of results on production costs

R.V. of pricing policy stockholding system } to accommodate changes

R.V. of ad hoc approaches to clients; (apparently) tailor-made offers — broadcast

R.V. of Advertizing programme by TV | Mag | Papers | Billboards | etc

amplifiers

stability criteria:
SALES OF
A —— 800 / 1000
B —— 740 / 800
... ——
Z —— 1600 / 1750

attenuators

R.V. of Basic Market Research Programme

R.V. of spot check research; activity sampling; e.g. interviews at airports

R.V Training of Market to limit demand e.g. 'any colour so long as it's black'.

R.V. of presentation of claimed benefits to client

R.V. of training of (? casual) interview staff

R.V. of accessibility; physiological capacity to assimilate

input transducers

higher variety bloc:
MARKET ENVIRONMENT
R.V. to match production

output transducers

R.V. of sampling process

R.V of answering format and comprehension

R.V of system's capability to detect results of special limitation

149

NOTE TO THE APPENDIX

Some Applications of the Viable System Model*

Applications of the V.S.M. by its author during the evolution and verification of the model have been so many and so widespread as to defy a proper listing. For the record, however, the range of amenable organizations ought to be indicated, leaving case histories to the published papers and books. Small industrial businesses in both production and retailing, such as an engineering concern and a bakery, come to mind; large industrial organizations such as the steel industry, textile manufacturers, shipbuilders, the makers of consumer durables, paper manufacturers are also represented. Then there are the businesses that deal in information: publishing in general, insurance, banking. Transportation has figured: railways, ports and harbours, shipping lines. Education, and health (in several countries), the operation of cities, belong to studies of services. Finally comes government at all levels — from the city, to the province, to the state and the nation-state itself — and the international agencies: the V.S.M. has been applied to several.

In this opening paragraph we have been talking of one man's work. Obviously then, these were not all major undertakings, nor is 'success' claimed for massive change. On the other hand, none of these applications was an academic exercise. In every case we are talking about remunerated consultancy, and that is not a light matter. The activities did not necessarily last for very long either, since speedy diagnosis is a major contribution of the whole approach. On the other hand, some of them have lasted for years. Undoubtedly the major use of this work to date was in Chile from 1971–73: five chapters ending the second edition of *Brain*[3] describe it in full. As this is written, however, a new undertaking on a similar scale is beginning in another country. On the question of what constitutes 'success' in consulting; reference may be made to Part Four, Note One of *Heart*.[4]

Of other people's work in the field of managerial cybernetics that has made application of the V.S.M., first mention must go to Raúl Espejo. He has given his own account of the 1971–73 Chilean application that we undertook together.[15] Since then, his teaching and research at Aston University in England has been centred on the V.S.M., and outcomes have been published in several articles and papers (especially Espejo[16,17]). His diagnoses have been profound, and he is adding to the corpus of theory.

The number of senior degrees, including doctorates, that have employed the V.S.M. under Espejo's direction is already in double figures. Professor David Mitchell's teaching has generated a similar

*Reprinted by kind permission from *J. Opl. Res. Soc.*, Vol. 35, No. 1, (Jan. 1984), pp. 23–5.

number of postgraduate theses using the V.S.M. at Concordia University in Quebec. Several more have emerged from Brunel University, under the direction of Professor Frank George. In the United States, Professors Richard Ericson and Stuart Umpleby (at George Washington University), Professor Barry Clemson (at the Universities of Maryland and of Maine), and Professor William Reckmeyer (at San José State University) have all made extensive use of this teaching, and others from Australia to India have reported similarly.

At Manchester University in the Business School, Geoffrey Lockett (directing the doctorial programme) has sponsored whole-week 'experiences' of the V.S.M.; and Professor Roger Collcutt has invented a unique pedagogic framework whereby M.B.S. students undertake projects to apply the V.S.M. to functional management, subsequently to merge the insights gained into a general management picture. Another novel development has been made by Ronald H. Anderton in the Systems Department of Lancaster University: practical applications of the V.S.M. in the form of project work have for some years been an important part of his *under*graduate teaching.

In the development of the technology that goes with the V.S.M. — the operations room, the computer programs, the financial regulatory systems, and so forth — the most outstanding progress since the work of the Chilean team more than a decade ago has been made by Robert Bittlestone, now the head of Metapraxis Ltd in England.

A veritable kaleidoscope of applications of the V.S.M. has been presented by Dr Paul Rubinyi in Canada. From penological systems to health services in the public sector, from oil companies to wheat cooperatives in the private sector, and from provincial planning to air transportation in federal government: every kind of organization has been mapped, in virtually continuous work over the last 13 years.

Other separate applications in Canada include the work of Walter Baker, Raoul Elias and David Griggs[18] on the Fisheries and Marine Service, which took unique advantage of managerial involvement, and that of Raoul Elias for Gaz Metropolitain. David Beatty has used the model for educational planning in Ontario, and I believe that it has been in independent action on the West Coast as well.

In Latin America, Professor Jorge Chapiro is a leading exponent of the V.S.M. who consults over the whole spectrum of industrial and governmental management in several countries.

In Australia, applications in an insurance company have been made by J. Donald de Raadt; in Switzerland Dr Peter Gomez[19] has used the V.S.M. in a publishing company, making an interesting experiment in melding this methodology with the 'root definitions' of Professor Peter

Checkland. In wider fields still we find a useful V.S.M. application in Finland by Dr S. Korolainen[20] to ekistics; and David Noor has published "A viable system model of scientific rationality" as a working paper from the University of Western Ontario.

On the strictly biological side, but not from the original neurophysiological perspective, Dr Richard Foss in England has made many mappings: for example, on the Eukaryote cell, the annual plant and the honeybee colony. He has found the V.S.M. to hold in such diverse systems; and he is extending the work to the slime mould *Dictyoltelium*, to lichens and to vertebrates, considering both the evolution and ontogeny of each system.

It does appear that the V.S.M. has sufficient generality to justify its origin as an attempt to discover *how systems are viable*; and that it also generates considerable power to describe and predict, diagnose and prescribe. No systematic archive of applications has been kept: perhaps it would be helpful to start one. These notes are compiled from such recollections and records as happen to be to hand.

REFERENCES

[1] S. Beer (1959) *Cybernetics and Management*. English Universities Press.
[2] S. Beer (1960) Towards the cybernetic factory. In *Principles of Self Organization*. Symposium of 1960, Pergamon Press, Oxford.
[3] S. Beer (1972) *Brain of the Firm*. Allen Lane, Penguin, Hardmondsworth.
[4] S. Beer (1979) *The Heart of Enterprise*. Wiley, Chichester.
[5] S. Beer (1981) *Brain of the Firm*, 2nd edn. Wiley, Chichester.
[6] S. Beer (1966) *Decision and Control*. Wiley, Chichester.
[7] S. Beer (1965) The world, the flesh and the metal. *Nature* **205** (No. 4968), 223–231.
[8] W. R. Ashby (1965) *Introduction to Cybernetics*. Chapman & Hall, London.
[9] G. Sommerhof (1950) *Analytical Biology*. Oxford University Press.
[10] C. Shannon and W. Weaver (1949) *The Mathematical Theory of Communication*. University of Illinois Press.
[11] S. Beer (1975) *Platform for Change*. Wiley, Chichester.
[12] S. Beer (1983) A reply to Ulrich's "Critique of pure cybernetic reason: the Chilean experience with cybernetics". *J. appl. Systems Analysis* **10**.
[13] F. Capra (1982) *The Turning Point*. Bantam Books, New York.
[14] *Brain and Strategy* **4** (No. 9), February 7th (1983).
[15] R. Espejo (1980) Cybernetic praxis in government: the management of industry in Chile 1970–1973. *J. Cybernetics* **10** (No. 3).
[16] R. Espejo (1978) Multi-organizational strategies; an analytical framework and case. In *Applied General Systems Research, Recent Developments and Trends* (G. Klir, Eds). Plenum Press, New York.
[17] R. Espejo (1980) Information and management: the cybernetics of a small company. In *The Information Systems Environment* (H. Lucas, F. Land, T. Lincoln and K. Supper, Eds). North Holland.
[18] W. Baker, R. Elias and D. Griggs (1978) Managerial involvement in the design of adaptive systems. In *Management Handbook for Public Administration* (J. W. Sutherland, Ed.). Van Nostrand Reinhold, New York.
[19] P. Gomez (1982) Systems metholody in action. *J. applied Systems Analysis* **9**.
[20] S. Korolainen (1980) *On the Conceptual and Logical Foundations of the General Theory of Human Organizations*. Helsinki School of Economics.